Briefly:
Sartre's *Existentialism and Humanism*

Already published in 'The SCM *Briefly* Series'

Briefly:
Sartre's *Existentialism and Humanism*

David R. Law

scm press

© David R. Law 2007

The Author has asserted his right under the Copyright, Designs and
Patents Act, 1988, to be identified as the Author of this Work

The author and publisher acknowledge material reproduced from
Existentialism and Humanism by Jean-Paul Sartre, translated by Philip
Mairet. Originally a 1946 lecture in French entitled *L'Existentialisme est
un Humanisme*. Copyright © 1996 by Editions Gallimard. Reprinted
by permission of Methuen Publishing Limited and Georges Borchardt,
Inc., for Editions Gallimard.

British Library Cataloguing in Publication data

A catalogue record for this book is available
from the British Library

978 0 334 04121 4

First published in 2007 by SCM Press
9–17 St Alban's Place
London N1 0NX

www.scm-canterburypress.co.uk

SCM Press is a division of
SCM-Canterbury Press Ltd

Typeset by Regent Typesetting, London
Printed and bound in Great Britain by
Bookmarque Ltd, Croydon, Surrey

Contents

Contents

In Memory of

Alan Robert Wardle

(1962–2006)

Introduction

The SCM *Briefly* series is designed to enable students and general readers to acquire knowledge and understanding of key texts in philosophy, philosophy of religion, theology and ethics. While the series will be especially helpful to those following university and A-level courses in philosophy, ethics and religious studies, it will in fact be of interest to anyone looking for a short guide to the ideas of a particular philosopher or theologian.

Each book in the series takes a piece of work by one philosopher and provides a summary of the original text, which adheres closely to it, and includes direct quotations from it, thus enabling the reader to follow each development in the philosopher's argument(s). Throughout the summary, there are page references to the original philosophical writing, so that the reader has ready access to the primary text. In the Introduction to each book, you will find details of the edition of the philosophical work referred to.

In *Briefly: Sartre's Existentialism and Humanism* we refer to Jean-Paul Sartre, *Existentialism and Humanism*, translated by Philip Mairet, London: Methuen, 1974, ISBN 041331300X.

Each *Briefly* begins with an Introduction, followed by a chapter on the Context in which the work was written. Who was this writer? Why was this book written? With Some Issues to Consider, and some Suggestions for Further Reading, this

Introduction

Briefly aims to get anyone started in their philosophical investigation. The detailed summary of the philosophical work is followed by a concise chapter-by-chapter Overview and an extensive Glossary of terms.

All words that appear in the Glossary are highlighted in bold type the first time that they appear in the Detailed Summary and the Overview of this *Briefly* guide. The Glossary also contains some terms used elsewhere in this *Briefly* series.

Context

Who was Jean-Paul Sartre?

Jean-Paul Charles Aymard Sartre, arguably the most famous of the existentialist philosophers, was born in Paris on 21 June 1905. He was an only child who lived with his young widowed mother and his maternal grandparents, who kept him isolated from other children until he was over ten years old. This unusual upbringing may have influenced his later writings, which frequently deal with human beings in isolation and alienation from others. After his studies at the École Normale Supérieure in Paris, during which he met and began his lifelong relationship with Simone de Beauvoir, Sartre taught philosophy at a school in Le Havre. In 1933–4 he interrupted his teaching career to spend a year at the French Institute in Berlin, where he immersed himself in the philosophy of Edmund Husserl.

Sartre's first major publication was *Nausea*, published in 1938. This novel, which was an overnight success, is an exploration of the contingency, absurdity and meaninglessness of existence, the experience of which causes Roquentin, the main character of the novel, the revulsion and sickness that gives the novel its title. The year after the publication of *Nausea* Sartre brought out a collection of short stories, named after the first and arguably most famous of them, *The Wall*. These stories explore such 'existentialist' themes as the meaning-lessness of human existence in the face of death, 'bad faith' and freedom, themes which Sartre continued to explore in his trilogy *Roads to Freedom* (1945–9).

From June 1940 to March 1941 Sartre was a prisoner-of-war. After his release he turned his attention to the theatre. This resulted in *The Flies* (1943) and *Huis Clos* ('No Exit') (1944), the latter of which established Sartre as a major playwright and which contains Sartre's famous comment that 'Hell is other people'. During this literary activity Sartre had continued to work on arguably his most significant philosophical work *Being and Nothingness*, which was published in 1943. In 1945 Sartre gave his now famous lecture 'Existentialism is a Humanism', a revised version of which was published in 1946.

After the Second World War Sartre underwent a political evolution which led him to become increasingly involved with the communist party. It is a matter of dispute whether this meant that Sartre abandoned existentialism or was seeking to integrate the existentialist concern with the individual with political engagement on behalf of the working class. After the war he edited *Les Temps Modernes*, a left-wing review de-voted to the literary and political issues of the day. In 1948 he published another influential lecture, *What Is Literature?*, in which he argued for a 'committed' literature which should serve as a tool in the liberation of society from oppression and exploitation. *Dirty Hands* (1948), *Nekrassov* (1955) and *The Condemned of Altona* (1959) bear witness to this concern with 'committed' literature.

From the 1950s Sartre's writing focused increasingly on defending communism against its critics, protesting against French policy in Indo-China and Algeria, the Russian invasion of Hungary in 1956 and Czechoslovakia in 1968, the

Vietnam War and American imperialism, and the govern-
ment's attempt to suppress the student revolution of the late
1960s. In 1960 he brought out his second major philosophical
work, *Critique of Dialectical Reason*, and in 1963 he published
his autobiographical *Words*. In 1964 Sartre turned down the
Nobel Prize for Literature on the grounds that accepting it
would turn him into an institution and compromise his integ-
rity as a writer. In 1971 he published a major study of Flaubert
entitled *The Family Idiot*. Sartre died on 15 April 1980.

What is *Existentialism and Humanism*?

Existentialism and Humanism originated as a lecture entitled
'Existentialism is a Humanism', given at *Le Club Maintenant*
('The Now Club') on 29 October 1945. It was intended to refute the charge made by some critics that existentialism is not
a humanism but a nihilistic philosophy advocating anguish
and despair.

   Existentialism and Humanism indicates how popular Sartre
and his brand of existentialism had become. The room at *Le
Club Maintenant* was full to bursting. Several people fainted
and a number of chairs were broken in the commotion. Sartre
had difficulty making himself heard and discussion was impossible. Sartre later repeated the lecture to a more select
gathering and engaged in debate with some members of the
audience. In the audience was the Marxist Pierre Naville,
who made some trenchant criticisms of Sartre's argument.
The debate between Sartre and Naville, along with comments
from some of the other participants, is printed as an appendix
to Sartre's lecture.

   Existentialism and Humanism is a simplified version of
the argument Sartre advanced with greater philosophical

precision in *Being and Nothingness* (1943), and is one of the most accessible introductions to existentialism. The simplicity and accessibility of *Existentialism and Humanism* have often resulted, however, in a misunderstanding of the more careful-ly nuanced position developed in *Being and Nothingness*. It is for this reason that Sartre later came to regard *Existentialism and Humanism* as a mistake. Regardless of Sartre's own view of *Existentialism and Humanism*, however, this little work has become the classic statement of existentialism and is probably the most read of all existentialist writings.

The English translation of Sartre's lecture was published in 1948 under the title *Existentialism and Humanism*. This is a slightly misleading title, since the French original is 'Exist-entialism is a Humanism'. There are also some problems with the English translation of some of Sartre's key concepts. The most serious of these is the translation of *mauvaise foi* as 'self-deception', rather than more accurately as 'bad faith'. Another problem is the translator's decision sometimes to translate 'subjectivité' not as *subjectivity*, but as *the subjective*. This creates the impression that Sartre is advocating subject-ivism, whereas his concern is in fact to focus on the freedom of the individual *subject*. For the sake of clarity we shall use the more literal translations, but will include the terms used in the English translation in square brackets and marked by the abbreviation 'ET' for 'English Translation'.

We have endeavoured to maximize the use of inclusive lan-guage without distorting Sartre's arguments. It has not always been possible, however, to translate all of Sartre's language into inclusive language. As an existentialist Sartre writes about the *individual* human being. To translate the male lan-guage he uses of the single individual into plural language, i.e. 'man' to 'human beings', 'he' to 'they', creates the impression of a collectivity and solidarity between human beings that is not present in Sartre's philosophy. For this reason we will retain the singular, but will write 's/he', 'him/herself', and 'his or her' wherever possible. When this policy would result in the piling up of personal and possessive pronouns, however, we shall reluctantly resort to the use of the simple 'he' or 'him' employed in the English translation of *Existentialism and Humanism*.

The text of *Existentialism and Humanism* is a continuous piece of prose. Although the publisher of the French original introduced subtitles into the margin of the text, these do not always do justice to the stages of Sartre's argument. To allow the reader to follow Sartre's argument more easily, we have introduced our own subheadings into the text to indicate the main themes of Sartre's lecture.

Sartre's purpose in *Existentialism and Humanism* is to defend existentialism against the claims that existentialism is a pessimistic bourgeois philosophy that offers human beings only despair. Sartre claims that far from being pessimistic, existentialism is an optimistic philosophy because it confronts human beings with *choice*.

After briefly dispensing with various ill-founded criticisms of existentialism, Sartre introduces what he considers to be the defining characteristic of existentialism, namely, the principle that 'existence precedes essence'. To understand what Sartre means by this phrase it is perhaps helpful to begin with the opposite formulation 'essence precedes existence'. By 'essence' Sartre seems to mean two things. First, 'essence' denotes the characteristics that make a thing what it is. Thus, to take his own example, a paper-knife is a device for opening letters, consisting of a sharp-tipped but otherwise blunt blade joined to a handle. These defining characteristics are

5

the paper-knife's 'essence'. They are why the paper-knife is a paper-knife and not a book, table, or stone, all of which have different 'essences'. Second, 'essence' denotes *purpose*. When making a paper-knife, the craftsman has a specific purpose in mind for the object he is making, namely opening letters. To speak of the essence of a thing is thus to state, first, that it has defining characteristics or a *nature* that make it what it is, and, second, that it has a *purpose*.

When a craftsman makes a paper-knife, he does so according to the notion of the paper-knife he has in his mind and constructs it so that it can fulfil the purpose of opening letters. In the case of the paper-knife, then, essence precedes existence. We can have the notion of the paper-knife in our minds and recognize the paper-knife's purpose without any reference to real, existing paper-knives. The craftsman first has a mental blueprint of a paper-knife, which he then follows when he brings the paper-knife into existence by making it in his workshop.

According to Sartre the religious believer conceives of God's relation to human beings as similar to the craftsman's relation to the paper-knife. Just as the craftsman has a blueprint and purpose in mind when he makes a paper-knife, so too does God have a blueprint and purpose in mind when he creates human beings. Even when we deny the existence of God, this belief in a blueprint for human beings persists in the idea that human beings share a common human nature. As an example of belief in a universal human nature Sartre cites Kant's view that all human beings – whether they live in the jungle or are middle-class westerners – share the same basic characteristics.

Sartre, however, is convinced that God does not exist, and therefore that there is no God-given blueprint and purpose that define what human beings are. Human beings *define* themselves. This is what Sartre means by his claim that in the case of human beings *existence precedes essence*. The human being is what he wills, and his conception of what he is comes *after* he has willed to become what he is. Sartre describes this as the 'first principle of existentialism'.

Sartre unfolds this first principle of existentialism by describing the human being as a 'project', by which he means that the human being is a being which propels itself by will and decision towards a future of his or her own choosing. This means that the principle of 'existence precedes essence' is closely connected with *responsibility*, not only for oneself but for *all* human beings. In an argument that strongly echoes Kant's notion of the categorical imperative, Sartre claims that when a human being chooses him or herself s/he simultaneously chooses for *all* human beings. This is because when we create ourselves through our choices we are choosing an image of what we believe all human beings ought to be. Sartre illustrates this point with the examples of a person deciding to join a trade union or getting married. A person who chooses to join a Christian rather than a communist trade union is affirming that resignation rather than resistance is how people should live their lives. Likewise, the person who decides to get married is affirming the validity of monogamy for all human beings.

Existentialism's concern with the allegedly pessimistic notions of anguish, abandonment and despair stems from this emphasis on responsibility. Anguish stems from the burden of being alone with one's responsibility. Those who deny this anguish are guilty of what Sartre calls 'bad faith', which is the failure of the individual to accept responsibility for his or her choices. To illustrate the connection between anguish and responsibility Sartre cites Abraham's belief that he had been commanded by God to sacrifice his son Isaac (Genesis 22), and the case of a woman convinced that God was communicating with her through her telephone. In both cases it is the individual's *decision* to understand these events as communications from God. There is no proof that can establish without doubt that it is indeed God who is speaking. It is the responsibility of taking such decisions without guidance that is the cause of anguish to the individual.

'Abandonment' expresses the human being's isolation in making the choices that define his or her existence. The human being is 'abandoned' because there is nothing outside him/herself to which the human being can appeal for guidance. There is no 'blueprint', no God-given human nature, and no purpose from which the human being can take his or her bearings. The human being is on his own and his essence and purpose are what he decides them to be. This means, Sartre stresses, that there is no determinism – the human being can never appeal to external factors to justify his actions. On the contrary, the human being is free. Indeed, for Sartre the human being *is* freedom. Because there are no objective rules to guide him, the human being must constantly choose and re-choose his values.

Sartre illustrates the nature of 'abandonment' by considering a young man who seeks advice from Sartre on whether he should stay with his mother or join the French resistance. Although the young man seems to be seeking guidance, his choice of adviser shows he has already chosen his course of action. For example, if a Christian asks a priest for guidance, he has already made his decision on what he should do according to whether he has chosen a priest who is on the side of the resistance or supports collaboration with the Nazis. This example shows that we cannot avoid choosing, even when we appear to be asking someone else to make the decision for us. Human beings cannot escape from their freedom. They are, as Sartre puts it, 'condemned' to be free. We might express Sartre's point by saying that the human being has no choice but to choose. 'Abandonment', then, means that we are alone with our decisions and must take sole responsibility for them.

The third existentialist concept to which Sartre devotes his attention is 'despair'. 'Despair' is Sartre's term for our acknowledgement and acceptance of our limitations. Much of life lies outside our control and no one – including God – is going to intervene to solve our problems for us. We are in 'despair' because there is nothing in which we can hope. This should not lead to quietism, however. We should not give up apathetically in the face of the obstacles that lie in our way, but should act as best we can in the circumstances in which we find ourselves. Despair, then, is not a negative phenomenon, but is an awareness of our limitations and should be met by the resolve to act despite these limitations. This courageous living without hope, Sartre claims, is what Descartes meant when he said 'Conquer yourself rather than the world'. For Sartre the human being is the sum of his or her actions and thus the human being *is* only in so far as s/he acts.

The accusation that existentialism is pessimistic is thus mistaken. On the contrary, existentialism is optimistic because it ascribes to human beings the freedom to choose what they shall be. Sartre concludes that it is not existentialism's pessimism but the strenuousness of its optimism that people find so off-putting, because existentialism does not allow the individual to blame his or her character on external factors such as heredity or environment, but attributes to each individual sole responsibility for what s/he has chosen to be.

The condemnation of existentialism for allegedly confining the human being within his or her subjectivity is another bad misunderstanding of existentialism. Sartre explains that the reason existentialism takes subjectivity as its point of departure is that, as Descartes has shown, our immediate sense of our own selves is the only truth of which we can be absolutely certain. Furthermore, since unlike materialistic theories it does not reduce human beings to objects, existentialism is the only philosophy which does justice to human dignity. Sartre emphasizes, however, that subjectivity should not be confused with a narrowly individualistic subjectivism which isolates the individual from his or her fellow human beings. In his immediate sense of himself each human being knows himself in relation to other human beings, who moreover play a role in the self-knowledge of each individual human being. Sartre points out that a human being cannot recognize him or herself as spiritual, wicked, or jealous, unless s/he is recognized as such by other human beings. This means that each individual exists in a world of inter-subjectivity in which he is confronted by other free individuals and within which he must choose himself.

That existentialism is not guilty of narrow subjectivism is further indicated by the fact that it affirms a 'human universality of condition'. Sartre is careful to distinguish this condition from the notion of a universal human nature. The human universality of condition consists not in a set of fixed characteristics but in the limitations which define the situation in which all human beings exist. As examples of such limitations Sartre cites work and death, which are features of every human being's life regardless of wealth and status. These limitations are *objective* in the sense that all human beings encounter them in the world. They are *subjective* in the sense that each individual human being must decide for himself how to shape his existence within the context of these limitations. What is absolute and universal is the act of choice by which each human being makes him or herself into what s/he has decided to become. Sartre stresses, however, that this absoluteness of choice does not mean that the cultural forms that result from the agglomeration of human choices are absolute. It is the individual's act of choosing that is absolute, not the type of humanity which the individual's choice brings into existence.

Sartre concedes that his argument does not completely refute the charge of subjectivism, and turns to address related objections levelled at existentialism. He rejects the charge that existentialism advocates gratuitous choice by repeating his point that in choosing for him or herself the human being also chooses the attitude s/he believes to be appropriate for all human beings. Furthermore, the human being always makes his or her choice in a concrete situation. Existentialism's insistence that in choosing for themselves in concrete situations human beings simultaneously choose for all of humankind means that although existentialism holds that human beings choose without reference to any *a priori* values, this choice is not an arbitrary but a *responsible* choice. Choice is like a work of art. Although there are no rules which dictate in advance how the artist should go about his work, values are nevertheless present in the coherence of the artwork and the way the finished piece expresses the artist's will to create. Like the artist creating a work of art, the human being's choice of values is a creative act, for he too does not know in advance what he should be, but becomes what he is through the choices he makes.

A second objection made against existentialism is that it is impossible to judge other people on existentialist principles.

Sartre admits that we cannot judge another person's *choice* of values, but he argues we can judge whether that individual acknowledges or refuses to accept responsibility for his or her choices. The person who refuses to accept responsibility by, for example, ascribing his actions to fate or heredity is denying his own freedom. Such a person is guilty of 'bad faith', which is the individual's refusal to accept his or her freedom and to take responsibility for the choices s/he has freely made.

The third objection is that existentialism does not take moral values seriously, since for the existentialist everything is a matter of personal choice. Sartre responds to this criticism by arguing that if there is no God, then the human being has no choice but to choose his own values. There is no one else who can do it for him and no one else who can imbue his life with meaning and value.

In the final pages of his book Sartre defends his view that existentialism is a humanism. Sartre rejects the form of humanism which attributes significance to the human race because of the distinguished deeds achieved by great people. This type of humanism is absurd, Sartre claims, because it assumes that there is such a thing as the human race in its entirety and ignores the fact that the human being is never finished but is always an ongoing project. The notion of humanism Sartre advocates understands the human being as a being which has the capacity to 'transcend' itself. Human beings do not have fixed, unchangeable natures but are able to surpass, exceed, and go beyond themselves by pursuing aims which they themselves invent and choose. This means there is no other universe except the universe of subjectivity, i.e., the universe human beings create for themselves. Thus by 'subjectivity' the existentialist does not mean subjectivism, but rather is affirming the insight that the human being is forever present in a human universe. This view of the human being as a relation of transcendence and subjectivity is humanism, Sartre claims, because the human being is the sole legislator for himself and because he alone must decide for himself.

The objections raised against existentialism by its critics are thus without foundation. Existentialism does not promote despair, but simply draws the conclusions that follow from the non-existence of God, namely that each human being must take responsibility for himself, must invent and choose his values, and act on those values. In conclusion, existentialism is not a doctrine of despair, but an optimistic doctrine of action.

Sartre's lecture was followed by a discussion with members of the audience. Like many such discussions the questions and answers are sometimes unclearly formulated and the debate is hampered by looseness of terminology. Nevertheless, the main points of criticism are apparent. One contributor suggests that anguish, abandonment and despair are merely occasional and temporary phenomena and not expressions of the deep-seated, constant state that Sartre claims accompanies the human being's choice of him or herself. Further questions concern the apparent lack of connection between existentialism and action, Sartre's use of the term 'humanism', and the validity of the existentialist notion of freedom. Is it appropriate for existentialists to call upon human beings to strive for freedom without stating a concrete goal towards which each human being should be striving? Why should existentialism refuse to give concrete guidance, and does its refusal not mean that it implicitly supports reactionary social and political positions? Furthermore, does existentialism's emphasis on subjectivity mean there can be no absolute, objective truth? Perhaps one of the most substantive issues that arises in the discussion is the viability of Sartre's distinction between 'human condition' and 'human nature'. Are these really distinct concepts or is 'human condition' merely a modification of the notion of human nature in light of the crises of the twentieth century?

Existentialism and Humanism is not a full, coherent presentation of Sartre's philosophy, but is rather a popular summary of what Sartre believes to be the central principles of existentialism. This accounts both for the book's appeal and for its weaknesses. Its appeal lies in its accessible and generally readable presentation of ideas Sartre treated in a more complex and overtly philosophical way in *Being and Nothingness*. Its weaknesses stem from the fact that the popular style of *Existentialism and Humanism* means that many key ideas are not fully explained and in some cases seem to contradict arguments advanced in *Being and Nothingness*. Despite these shortcomings, *Existentialism and Humanism* remains a significant work which repays careful reading. In an age in which human beings increasingly blame their faults and failures on their genes or social background, *Existentialism and Humanism* serves as a reminder of the responsibility each of us must take for our actions and for the sort of human being each of us has chosen to become. With his concept of radical freedom Sartre calls each of us to take responsibility for ourselves and, in doing so, for our fellow human beings.

Some Issues to Consider

- In what sense can it be said that 'existence precedes essence'? Does not the ability of human beings to choose themselves indicate that they possess a common essence or 'human nature', namely, the capacity to *choose*? Is Sartre himself not admitting as much when he states that the human being is freedom? In what way would it change Sartre's argument if we accepted that human beings have some sort of *a priori* essence?

- Is it true that human beings make themselves through their choices? Are human beings not also 'made' by their genetic inheritance, upbringing, social class, education, and the culture in which they live? Is it thus not an oversimplification to say that human beings create themselves through their choices?

- Are the choices that human beings make truly 'free'? Is it not the case that the choices human beings 'freely' make are at least in part prompted by their personal background and by the context in which they live? Choice is arguably never fully free, because human beings live in an environment which has already limited the range of choices available to them.

- Is Sartre right when he claims that once human beings have chosen themselves, their essence is not fixed, but can be revised and modified by future choices? There are two issues here. First, does it make sense to describe this fluid, mutable personhood as 'essence'? Second, surely there are choices we make which do indeed permanently determine our 'essence' with no possibility of future revision. The choice to give up sciences at school, for example, closes off a variety of possibilities for the young person and determines to a large extent the sort of human being that young person will become, namely, a non-scientist. It is true that such decisions can sometimes be reversed, but usually only with considerable will and great effort. The decisions we make build up a momentum that makes it increasingly difficult to change direction, even if we should choose to do so. And what are we to make of the 'choice' to become a murderer? This is a choice of a mode of being that cannot be revised by future decisions. Even if the murderer serves his punishment and from then on lives a blameless life, he still remains a murderer.

- Are human beings *always* responsible for their actions? Is the person suffering from mental illness or a psychological disorder responsible for these states? Can we really say that such a person is what he is as the result of his free decision? There is clearly no place in Sartre's thinking for the legal concept of 'diminished responsibility'.

- Must there not be some 'objective' criterion of what is good for all human beings, if I am to take responsibility for all humankind when choosing for myself?

- Is Sartre's argument that bad faith can be condemned as incoherent not an attempt to set up an objective criterion, despite his denial of all objective criteria? Why should the individual not 'choose' incoherence, if this is the choice he freely decides to make? How can we judge this to be bad faith, unless we elevate the notion of coherence to the status of an objective criterion? But then how could we justify such an objective criterion on the basis of Sartre's denial of all objective values?

- Christian existentialists such as Søren Kierkegaard, Gabriel Marcel and John Macquarrie have attempted to reconcile the existentialist emphasis on human freedom with belief in God. Is religious belief as incompatible with existentialism as Sartre would have us believe or is it possible to combine the existentialist emphasis on freedom with belief in God? Must belief in God, as Sartre implies, always be a violation of human freedom?

Suggestions for Further Reading

Jean-Paul Sartre, *Being and Nothingness: An Essay on Phenomenological Ontology*, trans. Hazel E. Barnes, London: Routledge, 1989.

Jean-Paul Sartre, *The Transcendence of the Ego: A Sketch for a Phenomenological Description*, trans. Andrew Brown, London: Routledge, 2004.

Jean-Paul Sartre, *Sketch for a Theory of the Emotions*, trans. Philip Mairet, London: Routledge, 2002.

Jean-Paul Sartre, *Nausea*, trans. Robert Baldick, Harmondsworth: Penguin, 1965.

Jean-Paul Sartre, *Huis Clos and Other Plays*, Harmondsworth: Penguin, 2000.

Jean-Paul Sartre, *The Wall*, trans. Andrew Brown, London: Hesperus, 2005.

Annie Cohen-Solal, *Jean-Paul Sartre: A Life*, trans. Anna Cancogni, New York: The New Press, 1985.

David Cooper, *Existentialism: A Reconstruction*, Oxford: Blackwell, second edition, 1999.

Arthur C. Danto, *Sartre*, London: Fontana, 1985.

Thomas Flynn, *Existentialism: A Very Short Introduction*, Oxford: Oxford University Press, 2006.

Christina Howells (ed.), *The Cambridge Companion to Sartre*, Cambridge: Cambridge University Press, 1999.

Gerald Jones, Daniel Cardinal, Jeremy Hayward, *Existentialism and Humanism: Jean-Paul Sartre*, London: John Murray, 2003.

John Macquarrie, *Existentialism*, London: Penguin, 1991.

Brian Masters, *A Student's Guide to Jean-Paul Sartre*, London: Heinemann, 1970.

Gregory McCulloch, *Using Sartre*, London: Routledge, 2001.

Iris Murdoch, *Sartre: Romantic Rationalist*, London: Chatto and Windus, 1987.

George Myerson, *Sartre's Existentialism and Humanism: A Beginner's Guide*, London: Hodder and Stoughton, 2002.

Stephen Priest, *Jean-Paul Sartre: Basic Writings*, London: Routledge, 2001.

Mary Warnock, *The Philosophy of Sartre*, London: Hutchinson, 1965.

Mary Warnock, *Existentialism*, Oxford: Oxford University Press, 1970.

Detailed Summary of Sartre's
Existentialism and Humanism

The Critique of Existentialism (pp. 23–6)

Several reproaches have been made against **existentialism**. First, existentialism has been accused of being 'an invitation to people to dwell in **quietism** of **despair**' (p. 23). Its critics claim that existentialism teaches that there are no solutions and that therefore all our actions in this world are 'entirely ineffective'. Furthermore, its emphasis on the futility of action indicates that existentialism is ultimately a contemplative philosophy. Since contemplation is a luxury that only the middle classes have the time for, the Communists have condemned existentialism as merely another '**bourgeois** philosophy'.

A second criticism of existentialism is that it has 'underlined all that is ignominious in the human situation', and ignores everything that belongs to 'the brighter side of human nature' (p. 23). Existentialism is further accused of 'leaving out of account the solidarity of mankind and considering man in isolation' (p. 23). This is an accusation that has been made by the Communists, who allege that the dependence of existentialism on the notion of 'pure **subjectivity**' derived from **Descartes'** principle of *cogito ergo sum* makes it 'impossible to regain solidarity with other men who exist outside of the self' (p. 23). Christians, on the other hand, have criticized existentialism because it denies 'the reality and seriousness of human affairs' (p. 23). They claim that existentialists 'ignore the commandments of God and all values prescribed as eternal' (p. 24) and teach that 'everyone can do what he likes'. The result of this denial of values is that existentialism has no criterion for distinguishing right from wrong.

Existentialism and Humanism is a reply to these criticisms. The lecture aims to show that existentialism is a doctrine that makes human life possible and, furthermore, is a doctrine 'which affirms that every truth and every action imply both an environment and a human subjectivity' (p. 24).

The 'essential charge' levelled at existentialism is that it overemphasizes 'the evil side of human life'. This has led some people to identify existentialism with ugliness and to accuse existentialism of being '**naturalistic**'. It is puzzling that people are scandalized and horrified by existentialism, 'for no one seems to be much frightened or humiliated nowadays by what is properly called naturalism' (p. 24). People who are untroubled by a novel like **Zola**'s *La Terre* 'are sickened as soon as they read an existentialist novel' (p. 24). Similarly, 'Those who appeal to the wisdom of the people – which is a sad wisdom – find ours sadder still' (p. 24). Yet there is much in popular wisdom that is cynical and presents a disillusioned view of human beings; e.g. 'Charity begins at home' or 'Promote a rogue and he'll sue you for damage, knock him down and he'll do you homage' (pp. 24–5). It is precisely the people who quote such 'dismal proverbs' and hold such a negative view of human nature, who 'complain that existentialism is too gloomy a view of things' (p. 25). The 'excessive protests' of such people indicate that it is not the pessimism but rather the *optimism* of existentialism that annoys them. What makes existentialism an optimistic doctrine and simultaneously makes it so alarming to some people is that 'it confronts man with a possibility of choice' (p. 25). To show this it is necessary to establish what existentialism is.

The problem is that the term 'existentialism' has been misunderstood and misused. Existentialism has become a fad and the term is employed by people with little knowledge of its real meaning (pp. 25–6). Those who seize on existentialism because they are 'eager to join in the latest scandal or movement', will be disappointed, however, 'For in truth this is of all teachings the least scandalous and the most austere: it is intended strictly for technicians and philosophers' (p. 26).

The attempt to arrive at a precise definition of existentialism is further hampered by the fact that there are *two* types of existentialism. First, there are the Christian existentialists such as **Karl Jaspers** and **Gabriel Marcel**. Second, there are the 'existential atheists', among whom we can count **Martin Heidegger** and the French existentialists. What both types of existentialist have in common 'is simply the fact that they believe that *existence* **comes before** *essence* – or, if you will, that we must begin from subjectivity [ET: the subjective]' (p. 26).

Existence Precedes Essence (pp. 26–8)

The meaning of the existentialist principle that 'existence comes before essence' is best explained by comparing the existence of the human being with the existence of an article of manufacture such as a book or a paper-knife (p. 26). The artisan who has made a paper-knife 'has paid attention, equally, to the conception of a paper-knife and to the pre-existent technique of production which is a part of that conception and is, at bottom, a formula' (p. 26). That is, the artisan has produced the paper-knife by making use of certain methods of

production and according to a certain plan, namely his intention to produce a knife capable of cutting paper. It is, after all,
inconceivable to 'suppose that a man would produce a paper-
knife without knowing what it was for' (p. 26). If we express
this in philosophical terms, we can say of the paper-knife 'that
its essence – that is to say the sum of the formulae and the
qualities which made its production and its definition possible – precedes its existence' (p. 26).

The principle that 'essence precedes existence' has been
applied by religious believers to human beings. When we
conceive of God as creator, we conceive of him as 'a supernal
artisan'. This means that the conception of the human being
in God's mind corresponds to the idea of the paper-knife in
the mind of the artisan. Like the artisan making a paper-knife,
'God makes man according to a procedure and a conception.'
Consequently, 'each individual man is the realisation of a certain conception which dwells in the divine understanding'
(p. 27). Even when the notion of God is suppressed, as was the
case, for example, in the philosophical **atheism** of the eighteenth century, the priority of essence over existence persists
in the belief that human beings possess a common human
nature. Belief in 'human nature' means believing that every
human being is 'a particular example of a universal conception, the conception of Man' (p. 27). **Kant** provides a good example of this belief in a universal human nature, for he goes
so far as to hold 'that the wild man of the woods, man in the
state of nature and the bourgeois are all contained in the same
definition and have the same fundamental qualities' (p. 27).
In Kant's thinking, then, 'the essence of man precedes that
historic existence which we confront in experience' (p. 27).

Atheistic existentialism, however, rejects the existence
of God, but holds that there is nevertheless 'at least one be-

ing whose existence comes before its essence, a being which exists before it can be defined by any conception of it' (p. 28). This is the human being. But what does it mean to say that existence precedes essence? It means 'that man first of all exists, encounters himself, surges up in the world – and defines himself afterwards' (p. 28). That is, the human being is not defined in advance. There is no blueprint that determines what sort of human being he or she *must* be. Consequently, 'there is no human nature, because there is no God to have a conception of it' (p. 28). It is neither a God-given plan nor a fixed, universal human nature, but the *individual human being* who decides what he or she will be. The human being is what he wills, and his conception of what he is comes *after* he has willed to become what he is. This is the 'first principle of existentialism', namely that, 'Man is nothing else but that which he makes of himself' (p. 28).

Subjectivity and Responsibility (pp. 28–30)

Those who reproach existentialism with 'subjectivity' – understood in a pejorative sense – fail to realize that this first principle of existentialism expresses the fact 'that man is of a greater dignity than a stone or a table' (p. 28). What 'existence precedes essence' means is 'that man is, before all else, something which propels itself towards a future and is aware that it is doing so' (p. 28). In short, the human being is 'a **project** which possesses a subjective life, instead of being a kind of moss, or a fungus or a cauliflower'. In contrast to all other things in the world, the human being exists through will and decision.

It is important to get clear, however, on what we mean when we speak of will and decision. Our understanding of these two crucial existentialist terms can be confused by the common view of the will as 'a conscious decision taken . . . after we have made ourselves what we are' (p. 28). Examples of such conscious decisions are joining a political party, writing a book, or getting married. But in such cases, 'what is usually called my will is probably a manifestation of a prior and more spontaneous decision' (p. 29). The sort of decision with which existentialism is concerned is much more fundamental, namely with the fundamental act of will by means of which the human being creates him or herself.

This means that the principle that 'existence precedes essence' is closely connected with responsibility: 'the first effect of existentialism is that it puts every man in possession of himself as he is, and places the entire responsibility for his existence squarely upon his own shoulders' (p. 29). This is not merely individual responsibility, however, but responsibility for all human beings. This point is important for understanding what existentialists mean by 'subjectivity'. This term has two meanings, namely 'the **freedom** of the individual subject' and that the human being 'cannot pass beyond human subjectivity' (p. 29). It is the latter meaning which is 'the deeper meaning of existentialism' (p. 29).

When a human being chooses him or herself s/he simultaneously chooses for *all* human beings. This is because when choosing himself the human being is choosing an image of human beings as s/he believes they ought to be. When we choose we always choose what we believe to be good, and nothing can be good for us unless it is good for all human beings. Consequently, in choosing ourselves we are taking responsibility for all human beings, for in fashioning our own individual image through this choice, we assume that 'that image is valid for all and for the entire epoch in which we find ourselves' (p. 29). Consequently, our responsibility is 'much greater than we had supposed, for it concerns mankind as a whole' (p. 29). For example, if I choose to join a Christian rather than a communist trade union, I affirm the belief that 'resignation is my will for everyone, and my action is, in consequence, a **commitment** on behalf of all mankind' (p. 30). Similarly, 'if I decide to marry and to have children, even though this decision proceeds simply from my situation, from my passion or my desire, I am thereby committing not only myself, but humanity as a whole, to the practice of monogamy' (p. 30). In short, in choosing myself I am choosing on behalf of all human beings and 'am creating a certain image of man as I would have him to be' (p. 30). Consequently, in taking responsibility for myself I simultaneously take responsibility for all human beings.

Once we have grasped the existentialist notion of the priority of existence over essence, and the responsibility this principle entails, we are in a position to understand what is meant by such other key existentialist terms as '**anguish**, **abandonment** and despair' (p. 30).

Anguish (pp. 30–2)

When existentialists state that human beings are in anguish they mean that when a human being chooses him or herself and in doing so acts as 'a legislator deciding for the whole of mankind', s/he 'cannot escape from the sense of complete and profound responsibility' (p. 30). The burden of the responsibility of legislating on behalf of all humankind is the cause of anguish to the human being.

There are, of course, many human beings who choose without any show of anguish and who do not seem to be troubled by the responsibility of legislating on behalf of all human-kind. This shows, however, not that they do not suffer from anguish, but that 'they are merely disguising their anguish or are in flight from it' (p. 30). But what of the individual who claims that he is choosing only for himself and is unconcerned about the significance of his choice for other human beings? If we ask such an individual what would happen if everyone behaved as he did, and he replied 'everyone does not do so', then he is guilty of **bad faith** [ET: self-deception], for 'one ought always to ask oneself what would happen if everyone did as one is doing' (pp. 30–1). Furthermore, such an individual reveals his anguish by his attempts to disguise it, for when he 'lies in self-excuse, by saying "Everyone will not do it", . . . the act of lying implies the universal value which it denies' (p. 31). That is, in stating his conviction that not everyone will carry out the actions he has chosen for himself, the individual has assumed the universal validity of the value from which he wishes to exempt himself. Such an individual 'must be ill at ease in his conscience' (p. 31).

The anguish of the choosing human being has been described by **Kierkegaard** in his portrayal of the anguish Abraham felt after the angel had commanded him to sacrifice his son. Abraham's anguish was due precisely to it being *his* choice to sacrifice Isaac. It was his choice, because he could have no proof that the angel was really an angel, or indeed that he was really Abraham. Similarly, if a hallucinating, mad woman claims she is receiving divine orders through the telephone, her interpretation of these orders as coming from God is *her* decision. The choice of obeying or disobeying the angel or the voice on the other end of the telephone is mine and mine alone. It is the responsibility of this choice and the fact that I receive no guidance in making this choice that causes me anguish. There is no proof or sign to convince me of the rightness of my choice. It is I alone who decides whether my choice of a course of action is good or bad. And yet when I make this choice it is as if the whole human race were watching me and regulating itself by my behaviour. It is this that is the cause of anguish, for every human being ought to ask him or herself, 'Am I really a man who has the right to act in such a manner that humanity regulates itself by what I do?' (p. 32). Any human being who does not ask this question of himself 'is dissembling his anguish' (p. 32).

This anguish does not lead to quietism or inaction, however, but is 'of the kind well known to all those who have borne responsibilities' (p. 32). For example, a military commander cannot but feel anguish when he makes a decision to launch an attack that will send several men to their deaths. This anguish is something experienced by all leaders, but it does not prevent them from acting. On the contrary, it is rather 'the very condition of their action, for the action presupposes that there is a plurality of possibilities, and in choosing one of these, they realise that it has value only because it is chosen' (p. 32). It is with this type of anguish, i.e. with anguish as a condition of action, that existentialism is concerned.

Abandonment (pp. 32–9)

By the term 'abandonment' existentialists 'only mean to say that God does not exist, and that it is necessary to draw the consequences of his absence right to the end' (pp. 32–3). This thinking through the absence of God to its logical and existential conclusion distinguishes existentialism from the secular **morality** formulated by certain French professors around 1880. Despite rejecting God as 'a useless and costly hypothesis', these professors nevertheless attempted to find an *a priori*, objective basis in the intelligibility of the world for the moral values of honesty, progress and humanity, which they regarded as essential for a law-abiding society (p. 33). This means that their rejection of God did not change anything. The same 'God-given' values are still regarded as binding on human beings, the only difference being that the source of these values is found not in God but in some other, non-religious objective source. The existentialist, on the other hand, does not find an alternative objective source of values to replace the absent God. On the contrary, s/he 'finds it extremely embarrassing that God does not exist, for there disappears with Him all possibility of finding values in an intelligible heaven' (p. 33). With the disappearance of God not only is the religious basis of moral values lost but *all* attempts to ground morality on an objective foundation are undermined: 'There can no longer be any good *a priori*, since there is no infinite and perfect consciousness to think it' (p. 33).

The fact there is no higher will to which human beings can turn for guidance, means that, 'It is nowhere written that "the good" exists, that one must be honest or must not lie, since we are now upon the plane where there are only men' (p. 33). **Dostoyevsky** identified the problem correctly, when he wrote: 'If God did not exist, everything would be permitted.' It is this insight that existentialism takes as its starting-point. If there is no God, the human being is 'abandoned' because there is nothing outside himself to give him guidance. Consequently, he alone must take responsibility for himself, for it is he alone who decides his actions. This is the consequence of the fact that for the human being in a Godless universe existence precedes essence. The human being will therefore 'never be able to explain [his] actions by reference to a given and specific human nature' (p. 34). This further means that 'there is no **determinism** – man is free, man *is* freedom' (p. 34). He is 'Condemned to be free. Condemned, because he did not create himself, yet is nevertheless at liberty, and from the moment that he is thrown into this world he is responsible for everything he does' (p. 34). There is nothing to which the human being can appeal to justify his actions. He himself must take sole responsibility. He cannot even appeal to passion, for 'the existentialist does not believe in the power of passion'. To claim that one has been swept away by a grand passion is to refuse to face up to one's responsibility and to the fact that 'man is responsible for his passion' (p. 34). Nor can the human being appeal to some sign to guide his actions, for each human being is responsible for the way he interprets the sign he takes to guide him. There is guidance neither from God, nor 'objective' morality, nor passion, nor signs. The human being is on his own and he alone must decide how he will act and take responsibility for that decision. For the existentialist, every human being 'without any support or help whatever, is condemned at every instant to invent man' (p. 34).

A good example of abandonment is provided by a young man who came seeking advice on whether he should stay with his mother, whose 'one consolation was in this young man' (p. 35), or join the French resistance to fight the Nazi occupation. This young man was 'confronted by two very different modes of action; the one concrete, immediate, but directed towards only one individual; and the other an action addressed to an end infinitely greater, a national collectivity, but for that very reason ambiguous – and it might be frustrated on the way' (pp. 35–6). The young man was thus confronted by the choice between two kinds of morality, namely 'the morality of sympathy' and 'personal devotion' against 'a morality of wider scope but of more debatable validity' (p. 36). There is no authoritative source of guidance to which he can turn to help him resolve this dilemma. Christianity provides no assistance because it merely preaches a doctrine of charity, love of neighbour, self-denial, and choosing the hardest way. But it provides no guidance on what is the hardest way and consequently cannot help the young man to decide between the two choices confronting him. No person and no ethical scripture can give him an answer *a priori* to the question of which road he should take. Nor is **Kantianism** of any assistance. According to the Kantian ethic we should never regard another human being as a means, but always as an end. The problem is that this commandment applies to both the choices facing the young man. If he chooses to stay with his mother he will be treating her as an end and not as a means, but in doing so he will also be treating as a means those fighting to liberate France on his behalf. The same applies, however, to the opposite choice. If the young man chooses to abandon his mother and join the French resistance, then he is treating his comrades in the resistance as the end and his mother merely as a means.

Confronted by such ambiguity and uncertainty one possible solution might be to trust one's feelings. What do my instincts tell me about which course of action I should take? This was the young man's solution to his dilemma. He asked himself whether his loyalty to his mother or his desire to join the resistance was stronger. Whichever feeling was stronger would be the guide to his decision on how to act. But this 'solution' confronts us with a new problem, namely 'how does one estimate the strength of a feeling?' (p. 37). As long as this feeling is not acted upon, it proves nothing. It is only when I have acted upon my feeling that 'the strength of this affection' is 'defined and ratified'. But if I prove the strength of my feeling by acting upon it, then I have *already* chosen my preferred course of action. Consequently, 'I find myself drawn into a vicious circle': feeling justifies my action, but I then appeal to my action to justify the feeling which prompted my action.

There is a further problem with basing action on feeling, namely, that it is difficult to distinguish a genuine feeling from a feeling that is merely play-acting. Again, whether one is play-acting or genuinely acting in response to one's feelings can be decided only by acting on one's feelings. But this again means that action becomes the guide to the genuineness of feeling, thereby undermining the attempt to make feeling the guide of action. Since 'feeling is formed by the deeds that one does', this means that 'I cannot consult it as a guide to action' (p. 37). Consequently, we must conclude that 'I can neither seek within myself for an authentic impulse to action, nor can I expect, from some ethic, formulae that will enable me to act' (p. 37).

It might be argued at this point, however, that it is indeed possible to seek guidance for one's actions. After all, the young man sought guidance by asking a professor for advice. But in reality the young man's choice of adviser indicates that he had already chosen which course of action he would take. For example, if you are a Christian and decide to consult a priest for guidance, you have already chosen your course of action according to whether you have chosen a priest who is on the side of the resistance or is a collaborator with the Nazis. The type of priest you choose determines beforehand the kind of advice you will receive. By your choice of priest you have already decided in advance the type of advice you wish to receive and the course of action you will take (pp. 37–8). In coming to an existentialist philosopher for guidance, the young man thus knew exactly what sort of advice he was going to receive, namely, 'You are free, therefore choose – that is to say, invent' (p. 38). There is 'no rule of general morality' to guide you. There are no signs to help you make your choice.

If the Catholic objects there are indeed signs which can guide us in our actions, then, again, all that this shows is that the Catholic objector has already made his choice. There is nothing in the 'signs' themselves that can give us guidance, for the Catholic's interpretation of the signs as signs is again due to his choice. A good example is provided by a Jesuit priest, who interpreted the severe setbacks of his childhood, an unsuccessful love-affair, and his failure to pass his military examination as a sign 'that he was not intended for secular successes' and that God was telling him to devote his life to religion. This interpretation of the events of his life as 'signs' of God's will, however, was the Jesuit's decision, and others could have interpreted these events quite differently and have become something quite different from a Jesuit priest, such as, for example, a carpenter or a revolutionary. It is the Jesuit and he alone who bears the entire responsibility for the interpretation of the events of his life as signs of God's will.

This is what existentialists mean by 'abandonment', namely that each of us decides our being. We have no guidance to help us. We are abandoned to our own devices and we alone take responsibility for our choices and actions, which is why abandonment is always accompanied by anguish (p. 39).

Despair (pp. 39–44)

By the term 'despair' existentialists mean 'we limit ourselves to a reliance upon that which is within our wills, or within

the sum of the probabilities which render our action feasible'
(p. 39). That is, despair means living within one's possibilities
and acting on those possibilities. Since 'there is no God and
no prevenient design, which can adapt the world and all its
possibilities to my will', one can rely only on oneself. This was
Descartes' point when he said, 'Conquer yourself rather than
the world', by which he means that 'we should act without
hope' (p. 39). This reliance on one's own will, the limitation
of oneself to the possibilities contained in one's will, and the
call to conquer oneself rather than the world, are all *despair*
because they require us to give up hope in another power
to shape our lives for us. We are in despair, because there is
nothing in which we can hope.

A Marxist might object at this point that although it is true
that each individual's action is ultimately limited by his or her
death, the individual can rely on the help of others 'to take
up your action and carry it forward to its final accomplish-
ment which will be the revolution' (p. 39). Indeed, the Marxist
would argue that not to rely on one's comrades to continue
the struggle is immoral. But to rely on one's comrades in this
way is similar to relying on the train arriving on time or the
tram not being derailed when waiting for a friend to arrive.
I count on my comrades, 'in so far as they are committed, as
I am, to a definite, common cause; and in the unity of a party
or a group which I can more or less control – that is, in which
I am enrolled as a militant and whose movements at every
moment are known to me' (p. 40). That is, the action of my
comrades belongs to the probabilities of my life which I take
into consideration in deciding on my own actions. I cannot
rely, however, on human beings whom I do not know, nor can
I rely 'upon human goodness or upon man's interest in the
good of society' (p. 40). This is because each human being 'is

free' and furthermore, 'there is no human nature which I can take as foundational' (p. 40). Consequently, it is impossible for me to know whether the Russian Revolution will lead to the triumph of the proletariat, nor can I be sure that my comrades will take up and complete my work. My comrades are all 'free agents and will freely decide, to-morrow, what man is then to be' (p. 40). This impossibility of guaranteeing that my actions will be taken up and carried forward by others should not lead me to abandon myself to quietism, however. I should continue to commit myself and act on my commitments. I may even join a political party. But in committing myself, 'I should be without illusion and . . . I should do what I can' (p. 41). The success or failure of my ventures does not lie in my hands, but it is my task to do what I can.

This is far removed from quietism, which 'is the attitude of people who say, "let others do what I cannot do"' (p. 41). Existentialism does not advocate passing on responsibility for action to others; on the contrary, existentialism calls upon human beings to act without regard for the success or failure of their actions. It declares that 'there is no reality except in action'. Indeed, the precept of existentialism is, 'Man is nothing else but what he purposes, he exists only in so far as he realises himself, he is therefore nothing else but the sum of his actions, nothing else but what his life is' (p. 41).

This is why some people are horrified by existentialism. They are horrified because it confronts them starkly with their responsibility for the lives they lead. Because action is everything and is what makes the human being what he or she is, existentialism leaves no hiding place for the individual. I cannot excuse my failure to have had a great love, written a book, or had children by claiming that the circumstances were against me. Nor can I claim that I possess the ability to do all of these things and therefore have 'a worthiness that could never be inferred from the mere history of my actions' (p. 41). Existentialism rejects such excuses because 'there is no love apart from the deeds of love; no potentiality of love other than that which is manifested in loving, there is no genius other than that which is expressed in works of art' (p. 41). Although this existentialist teaching may seem comfortless to the person who has not made a success of his or her life, it confronts everyone with the fact that only action is reality, and that everything else – dreams, expectations and hopes – are delusions. In short, existentialism teaches that the human being 'is no other than a series of undertakings, that he is the sum, the organisation, the set of relations that constitute these undertakings' (p. 42).

In fact, what people are really reproaching existentialism for when they accuse it of pessimism is 'the sternness of our optimism' (p. 42). People condemn existentialist novels because, unlike Zola, existentialist writers do not ascribe the characters' baseness, weakness and cowardice to such external factors as heredity or environment, but attribute these vices solely and exclusively to the characters themselves. The coward, for example, is portrayed by the existentialist 'as responsible for his cowardice'. He has not been made a coward 'through his physiological organism', nor is there such a thing as 'a cowardly temperament'. The coward is a coward 'because he has made himself into a coward by his actions' (p. 43).

It is existentialism's attribution of responsibility to the individual that people find so disturbing. They sense that existentialists present the coward as being *guilty* of his cowardice. This is disturbing because, 'what people would prefer would be to be born either a coward or a hero' (p. 43). If people could attribute their cowardice or heroism to the way they were born, then they could absolve themselves of responsibility for their actions, for they could do nothing about their actions. They were simply born that way and are merely following their given nature. The existentialist rejects this view as a denial of responsibility and openly confronts the individual with his responsibility for his actions.

The reproaches made against existentialism are thus unfounded. Existentialism is not a philosophy of quietism, nor does it have a pessimistic view of human beings, nor does it discourage human beings from action. On the contrary, existentialism is 'an ethic of action and self-commitment' (p. 44).

Inter-Subjectivity (pp. 44–6)

A further criticism levelled against existentialism is that it is guilty of 'confining man within his individual subjectivity' (p. 44). This is again a bad misunderstanding of existentialism, for two reasons. First, existentialists take subjectivity as their point of departure not because they are 'bourgeois', but because they seek to base their teaching on the truth. This truth is the truth that '*I think, therefore I am*, which is the absolute truth of consciousness as it attains to itself' (p. 44). Any theory which does not take as its starting-point the individual's self-consciousness 'suppresses the truth, for outside of the **Cartesian** *cogito*, all objects are no more than probable' (p. 44). For there to be any truth, there must be an absolute truth. The only absolute truth that is 'easily attained and within the reach of everybody' is 'one's immediate sense of one's self' (p. 44). Subjectivity, then, is the necessary starting-point for thinking because our own existence is the only truth of which we can be absolutely certain.

Second, existentialism is the only philosophy which is compatible with human dignity, for 'it is the only one which does not make man into an object' (p. 45). Thus in contrast to **materialistic** theories, which reduce human beings to mere things, existentialism seeks 'to establish the human kingdom as a pattern of values in distinction from the material world' (p. 45).

A further point to note is that the existentialist conception of subjectivity 'is no narrowly individual subjectivism', for 'it is not only one's own self that one discovers in the *cogito*, but those of others too' (p. 45). There is a difference between Cartesian, Kantian and existentialist notions of subjectivity. In contrast to the philosophy of Descartes and Kant, the existentialist understanding of the *cogito* includes the presence of other selves. This is because the human being knows him or herself not as an isolated self but as a self in relation to other selves. Furthermore, the human being 'recognises that he cannot be anything . . . unless others recognise him as such' (p. 45). For example, he cannot recognize himself as spiritual, wicked, or jealous, unless he is recognized to be so by other human beings. Other human beings play a vital role in the self-knowledge of each individual human being. Consequently, 'I cannot obtain any truth whatsoever about myself, except through the mediation of another' (p. 45). This discovery of myself through my relationship with another person 'is at the same time the revelation of the other as a freedom which confronts mine, and which cannot think or will without doing so either for or against me' (p. 45). That is, human beings live in a world characterized by '**inter-subjectivity**' (p. 45). It is in relationship with others in this world of inter-subjectivity that each individual 'has to decide what he is and what others are' (p. 45).

The Human Condition (pp. 46–7)

Despite the fact that there is no universal human nature, there is 'a human universality of *condition*' (p. 46). This universal human condition consists of 'all the *limitations* which *a priori* define man's fundamental situation in the universe' (p. 46). Whether a person is born a slave, feudal baron, or proletarian, what will remain constant in these radically different lives are 'the necessities of being in the world, of having to labour and to die there' (p. 46). Despite the widely differing historical circumstances in which human beings live, they thus share a universal human condition.

The limitations of human existence are both subjective and objective. They are objective 'because we meet with them everywhere and they are everywhere recognisable' (p. 46). They are at the same time subjective, however, 'because they are *lived* and are nothing if man does not live them' (p. 46). That is, they are subjective because each and every individual human being must 'freely determine himself and his existence in relation to them' (p. 46). A further indication of a universal human condition is that no human purpose is wholly foreign to other human beings, 'since every human purpose presents itself as an attempt either to surpass these limitations, or to widen them, or else to deny or to accommodate oneself to them' (p. 46). Even if we do not ourselves adopt purposes chosen by other people, we can nevertheless acknowledge these purposes as human beings' attempts to live in relation to their objective limitations. Consequently, 'In every purpose there is universality, in this sense that every purpose is comprehensible to every man' (p. 46). No purpose defines a human being for ever, however, for a human being can always decide to choose him or herself anew. Consequently, although there is a human universality, 'it is not something given', but 'is being perpetually made' (p. 47). The universal human condition consists of the task of choosing oneself within the limitations imposed by human existence, but, 'This absoluteness of the act of choice does not alter the relativity of each epoch' (p. 47).

Commitment, Choice and Bad Faith (pp. 47–54)

Central to existentialism is 'the absolute character of the free commitment, by which every man realises himself in realising a type of humanity' (p. 47). It is only this commitment that is absolute, not the forms in which the human being expresses his or her commitment. The cultural forms which human beings' commitment and choices may create are always only relative. This means there is no difference between free being and absolute being. Free being is 'being as self-commital, as existence choosing its essence'. This free being is also 'absolute' being, because self-commitment and self-choice are fundamental and universal to all human beings. Consequently, 'there is no difference whatever between being as an absolute, temporarily localised – that is, localised in history – and universally intelligible being' (p. 47). Absolute being and universally intelligible being are identical, because every human being can recognize and understand the absoluteness of the commitment of every other human being, even though every human commitment always takes place in a concrete historical context and leads to a temporally localized form of being.

This argument, however, 'does not completely refute the charge of subjectivism' (p. 47), as can be seen from the fact that this charge reappears in new guises. First, existentialism stands accused of advocating anarchy because it allegedly teaches 'it does not matter what you do' (p. 47). Second, existentialism stands accused of having no standards to judge between right and wrong, for, the critic claims, 'You cannot judge others, for there is no reason for preferring one purpose to another' (p. 47). A third accusation is: 'Everything being merely voluntary in this choice of yours, you give away with one hand what you pretend to gain with the other' (p. 48). None of these accusations should be taken seriously. The first criticism, namely, that it does not matter what one chooses, fails to recognize the seriousness of choice. The seriousness of choice is indicated by the fact that it is impossible *not to choose*. Even if I choose not to choose, that is itself a choice. It is important to recognize this point, because it brings to our attention the fact that choosing takes place in a real situation and imposes 'a limit to fantasy and caprice' (p. 48). For example, the fact that I am a sexual being capable of having sexual relations and producing children confronts me with the demand to choose my attitude to this situation. Furthermore, in choosing this attitude I am simultaneously choosing for all humankind, for in choosing one course of action over another I am implicitly affirming my conviction that this is the way *all* human beings should behave. Since in choosing for myself I am choosing for all human beings, my choice is not arbitrary or capricious, because it is always accompanied by my responsibility for others. There is thus a fundamental difference between the existentialist notion of choice and **André Gide**'s theory of the gratuitous act. Gide's capriciousness is due to his failure to recognize that the human being always chooses *in a situation*. In contrast to Gide, the existentialist recognizes that the human being 'finds himself in an organised situation in which he is himself involved: his choice involves mankind in its entirety, and he cannot avoid choosing'

(p. 48). The human being cannot avoid choosing, for the decision not to marry and have children, for example, is itself a choice for which s/he must take responsibility. Consequently, although existentialism holds that the human being 'chooses without reference to any pre-established values', it is unjust to accuse existentialists of advocating arbitrary choice.

The nature of existential choice is best understood by comparing it with 'the construction of a work of art' (p. 48). This should not be taken to mean that existentialism affirms an 'aesthetic morality' (p. 49), but only that art provides a useful way of grasping what is distinctive about the existentialist notion of choice. No one reproaches an artist for not painting a picture according to *a priori* rules, nor do we define in advance what picture the artist should paint. It is the artist who decides what and how s/he will paint. Furthermore, although 'there are no aesthetic values *a priori*' (p. 49), values are nevertheless present in a work of art, namely, 'in the coherence of the picture, in the relation between the will to create and the finished work' (p. 49). In addition, we cannot know in advance 'what the painting of to-morrow will be like' (p. 49), nor can we judge a painting until it is finished.

A similar state of affairs pertains to morality. Like art, morality is a creative and inventive act. In morality, 'we cannot decide *a priori* what it is that should be done' (p. 49). This has already become clear in the case of the young man seeking advice on whether he should stay with his mother or join the resistance. He was unable to find any sort of guidance and consequently 'was obliged to invent the law for himself' (p. 49). In neither course of action open to him could we accuse him of choosing moral irresponsibility. What this example shows is that the human being 'makes himself; he is not found ready-made; he makes himself by the choice of his morality' (p. 50).

And the human being cannot avoid this self-creative choice of morality, for he constantly lives in a situation that demands s/he choose. The insight of existentialism is that the human being is defined 'only in relation to his commitments'. Consequently, the charge of irresponsibility levelled by the critics of existentialism is simply 'absurd' (p. 50).

The second objection levelled against existentialism is that it is impossible to judge others on existentialist principles. This is both true and false. It is true because 'whenever a man chooses his purpose and his commitment in all clearness and in all sincerity, whatever that purpose may be it is impossible to prefer another for him' (p. 50). It is true also because existentialists 'do not believe in progress'. 'Progress implies amelioration' (p. 50), but existentialists believe that the human being is always the same. Although the situation in which human beings find themselves may change, human beings and the task of making a choice in whatever situation human beings find themselves do not change. In short, the moral problem facing human beings always remains the same.

In another sense, however, the critic is wrong, for it is indeed possible to judge others on the basis of existentialist principles. Judgement of others is possible because, as said earlier, 'one chooses in view of others, and in view of others one chooses himself' (p. 50). First, one can make a judgement, not of value but of logic, that 'in certain cases choice is founded upon an error, and in others upon the truth' (p. 50). Thus one can judge someone by saying that s/he is guilty of bad faith [ET: self-deception]. If human beings live in a situation of free choice, then any human being who attempts to absolve himself of the responsibility of choice by appealing to his passions 'or by inventing some deterministic doctrine' (p. 51) is guilty of bad faith, because he has refused to take responsibility for the choices he has freely made. But an objector might ask why a human being should not choose bad faith, if he so desires. There are two responses to this objection. First, the judgement that someone is guilty of bad faith is not a moral judgement, but a logical judgement, namely that the individual is guilty of inconsistency. He has freely chosen, but wishes to acknowledge neither his freedom nor his choice. Thus bad faith 'is evidently a falsehood, because it is a dissimulation of man's complete liberty of commitment' (p. 51). Consequently, 'one cannot avoid pronouncing a judgment of truth' (p. 51). Another example of bad faith is when I claim I am *obliged* to observe certain values. If I claim this I am contradicting myself, for I am simultaneously claiming, on the one hand, that I will freely choose certain values and, on the other hand, that these values 'impose themselves upon me' (p. 51). If someone then asks what is wrong with his or her wishing to choose bad faith, then my reply is that although there is no reason why that person should not choose bad faith, I nevertheless may declare his choice to be bad faith and point out that 'the attitude of strict consistency alone is that of good faith' (p. 51). This, then, is the first way the existentialist can judge the person of bad faith: he can show that the behaviour of such a person is inconsistent and self-contradictory, and therefore is a logical error.

The second response to the question 'Why should a person not choose bad faith?' is to pass a moral judgement. This moral judgement stems from the fact that 'freedom, in respect of concrete circumstances, can have no other end and aim but itself' (p. 51). The person of good faith 'can will only one thing, and that is freedom as the foundation of all values', for he knows that values depend upon himself and upon his freely made choices. This recognition and willing of freedom as the foundation of all values means that 'the actions of men of good faith have, as their ultimate significance, the quest of freedom itself as such' (p. 51). This is the existentialist aim, namely 'to will freedom for freedom's sake', not abstractly, but 'in and through particular circumstances' (p. 51). This does not isolate us from other human beings, however, for 'in thus willing freedom, we discover that it depends entirely upon the freedom of others and that the freedom of others depends upon our own' (pp. 51–2). My freedom and the freedom of others are intimately connected. This stems from the concrete nature of freedom. When freedom is understood only abstractly, 'freedom as the definition of a man does not depend upon others'. But when I understand freedom in concrete terms as an act of commitment in a particular, concrete situation, then 'I am obliged to will the liberty of others at the same time as mine' (p. 52). That is, because when I choose, I choose what I believe to be the right choice for *all* human beings, 'I cannot make liberty my aim unless I make that of others equally my aim' (p. 52).

The authentic human being is thus 'a being whose existence precedes his essence' (p. 52), who is free and freely wills his freedom in all circumstances in which he finds himself. When I recognize this, I simultaneously realize that I must will not only my own freedom but also the freedom of others. It is this recognition of the primacy of freedom for *all* human beings that enables me to pass judgement on the person of bad faith. Such judgement is undertaken 'in the name of that will to freedom which is implied in freedom itself'. For the sake of freedom, the existentialist judges those who seek to flee from their freedom and 'hide from themselves the wholly voluntary nature of their existence and its complete freedom' (p. 52). Those who hide from their freedom 'in a guise of solemnity or with deterministic excuses' are 'cowards' (p. 52). Those who claim that their existence is necessary when in fact 'it is merely an accident of the appearance of the human race on earth' are 'scum' (p. 52). 'Cowards' and 'scum' can be identified, however, only 'upon the plane of strict **authenticity**' (p. 52). This means that 'although the content of morality is variable, a certain form of this morality is universal' (p. 52). Kant was right in declaring that 'freedom is a will both to itself and to the freedom of others' (p. 52), but he mistakenly believed that 'the formal and the universal suffice for the constitution of a morality' (p. 52). Existentialists, on the other hand, hold that 'principles that are too abstract break down when we come to defining action' (p. 52). Again, the student who is struggling to decide whether to stay with his mother or join the resistance provides a good example. What are the criteria according to which the young man could make his decision? The problem is there is no 'authority', no 'golden rule of morality' that can help him decide. There are simply 'no means of judging' (p. 52). There is no abstract principle to which the student can appeal to guide him in his decision. Consequently, the 'content' of the decision is 'always concrete, and therefore unpredictable' (pp. 52–3). The content 'has always to be invented'; that is, the individual decides not according to some abstract principle but always within the confines of the concrete situation in which he finds himself. We cannot judge the content of the decision, but what is important 'is to know whether the invention is made in the name of freedom' (p. 53).

Two examples from nineteenth-century literature can help throw light on this issue. Maggie Tulliver of **George Eliot**'s *Mill on the Floss* is a passionate woman who is in love with a man who is engaged to someone else. Despite her passion

Maggie decides to renounce her happiness and 'chooses in the name of human solidarity to sacrifice herself and to give up the man she loves' (p. 53). The character of La Sanseverina in **Stendhal**'s *Chartreuse de Parme* would act quite differently if she found herself in Maggie Tulliver's position. Convinced it is passion that endows the human being with true value and significance, La Sanseverina would choose in the name of passion to sacrifice not her own happiness but that of her rival. In these two novels, then, we would seem to be faced by two opposing moralities. If we look more closely, however, we see that despite their differences the two moralities espoused by Maggie Tulliver and La Sanseverina are 'equivalent', for 'in both cases the overruling aim is freedom' (p. 53). The central role of freedom is further indicated if we compare two other cases that might appear to be identical to those of Maggie Tulliver and La Sanseverina. At first sight the behaviour of the girl who gives up her love in resignation and that of the girl who chooses 'in fulfilment of sexual desire, to ignore the prior engagement of the man she loved' (p. 53), might seem to correspond respectively to the moral positions of the two women of Eliot's and Stendahl's novels. This is merely an external similarity, however, for in fact the actions of the two girls are 'entirely different'. Maggie Tulliver and La Sanseverina act on the basis of their free choice of the principles of human solidarity and the primacy of passion, and consequently 'the attitude of La Sanseverina is much nearer to that of Maggie Tulliver than to one of careless greed' (pp. 53–4). From these considerations we can see that the objection that it is impossible to judge others on existentialist principles 'is at once true and false' (54). The examples of Maggie Tulliver and La Sanseverina show that 'One can choose anything, but only if it is upon the plane of free commitment' (p. 54).

The third objection, namely that everything is voluntary in existentialism, is tantamount to the accusation 'your values are not serious, since you choose them yourselves' (p. 54). The only reply that can be made to this charge is, 'I am very sorry that it should be so; but if I have excluded God the Father, there must be somebody to invent values' (p. 54). In short, if there is no God, then human beings have no choice but to choose their own values. To accept that human beings must invent their values is to affirm 'there is no sense in life *a priori*'. Life is what we make of it. Indeed, 'Life is nothing until it is lived; but it is yours to make sense of, and the value of it is nothing else but the sense that you choose' (p. 54). This makes clear that existentialism recognizes the 'possibility of creating a human community' (p. 54).

Existentialism is a Humanism (pp. 54–6)

The claim that existentialism is a **humanism** has been challenged in some quarters. It has been furthermore pointed out that *Nausea* contains a critique of humanism. To argue that existentialism is a humanism, it is claimed, constitutes a retraction of the critique of humanism stated in *Nausea*. This criticism is based, however, on a failure to distinguish between two different meanings of humanism. The first type of humanism is 'a theory which upholds man as the end-in-itself and as the supreme value' (p. 54). A good example of this type of humanism can be found in **Jean Cocteau**'s *Round the World in 80 Hours*. As one of the characters is flying over mountains in an aircraft, he exclaims, full of admiration for the technical achievement of flight, 'Man is magnificent!' To make such a statement is to attribute to myself, by virtue of my being a member of the human race, the achievements of other human beings. The thinking behind this view is that 'we can ascribe value to man according to the most distinguished deeds of certain men' (p. 55). This kind of humanism is 'absurd' (p. 55) and inadmissible. It is absurd, 'for only the dog or the horse would be in a position to pronounce a general judgement upon man and declare that he is magnificent, which they have never been such fools as to do' (p. 55). It is inadmissible, because no human being can pronounce judgement on the human race as such, for this assumes there is such a thing as the human race in its entirety. Consequently, 'Existentialism dispenses with any judgement of this sort: an existentialist will never take man as the end, since man is still to be determined' (p. 55). Furthermore, 'we have no right to believe that humanity is something to which we could set up a cult'. To do so would ultimately lead to fascism.

The second meaning of humanism, on the other hand, is that 'Man is all the time outside of himself: it is in projecting and losing himself beyond himself that he makes man to exist; and, on the other hand, it is by pursuing transcendent aims that he himself is able to exist' (p. 55). That is, the human being has the capacity to go beyond himself, and does so by pursuing aims that he himself invents and chooses. There is thus 'no other universe except the human universe, the universe of human subjectivity' (p. 55), i.e. the universe that human beings create for themselves. This provides us with the basis for understanding *existential humanism*. Existential humanism consists of the 'relation of **transcendence** as constitutive of man . . . with subjectivity' (p. 55). We must, however, get clear on what we mean by 'transcendence' and 'subjectivity' here. By 'transcendence' the existentialist does not mean 'the sense in which God is transcendent', but uses the term to express the capacity of human beings to surpass, exceed and go beyond themselves. By 'subjectivity' the existentialist does not mean subjectivism, i.e. the view that the human being is 'shut up in himself', but employs the term to express that the human being is 'forever present in a human universe' (p. 55). This view of the human being as a relation of transcendence with subjectivity is *humanism*, because *the human being* is the sole legislator for himself and because 'he himself, thus abandoned, must decide for himself' (p. 56). Furthermore, existentialism is a humanism, because it makes clear that it is 'always by seeking, beyond himself, an aim which is one of liberation or of some particular realisation, that man can realise himself as truly human' (p. 56).

In conclusion, the objections raised against existentialism are unjust. Existentialism is simply 'an attempt to draw the full conclusions from a consistently atheistic position' (p. 56). It does not aim to plunge human beings into despair. The existentialist conception of despair is different from the Christian understanding, which conceives of despair as 'any attitude of unbelief'. The atheism of existentialism is due not to demonstrating that God does not exist, but to the conviction that even if God did exist, it would make no difference to the existentialist. The real problem is not the existence or non-existence of God but that 'nothing can save [the human being] from himself, not even a valid proof of the existence of God' (p. 56). That is, each human being must take responsibility for himself, must invent and choose his values, and act on those values. Consequently, far from being a doctrine of despair, 'existentialism is optimistic, it is a doctrine of action, and it is only by bad faith [ET: a self-deception], by confusing their own despair with ours that Christians can describe us as without hope' (p. 56).

Sartre's Discussion with Members of the Audience (pp. 57–70)

The first questioner's main point is that such terms as despair, abandonment and anguish refer to 'a state of consciousness of the human predicament which does not arise all the time' (p. 57). The questioner concedes that in the act of choice 'one is choosing whom one is to be', but argues that 'anguish and despair do not appear concurrently' (p. 57).

Sartre responds by first making clear that in speaking of choice he is not concerned with such trivialities as the choice between a vanilla slice and a chocolate éclair. When he states that anguish is a constant feature of the human being's life, he means it in the sense 'my original choice is something constant'. This anguish stems from 'the complete absence of justification at the same time as one is responsible in regard to everyone' (p. 57). Sartre's point is that an individual's past choice to become the sort of person s/he now is, is a decision that continues to reverberate in the present precisely because that past decision is what has made that person what s/he now is. This means that anguish is constant, first, because the person the individual is, continues to be without any objective justification and, second, because the human being continues to be responsible to the whole of humanity in continuing to live according to his or her past decision to become the human being s/he now is.

The questioner replies by telling Sartre he was referring to Sartre's essay in the journal *Action*, 'in which it seemed to me that your own point of view was somewhat weakened' (p. 57). Sartre attributes this apparent weakening of his argument to his being asked questions by people who are not qualified to do so. He was thus 'presented with two alternatives, that of refusing to answer or that of accepting discussion upon the level of popularisation' (p. 57). Sartre chose the path of popularization, for it is 'not such a bad thing' to consent 'to some weakening of an idea in order to make it understood' (p. 58). Sartre further points out that since existentialist philosophy is a philosophy of commitment 'which says that existence precedes essence, it must be lived to be really sincere' (p. 58). This means that it is not enough to describe existentialism in books, for 'if you want this philosophy to be indeed a commitment, you have to render some account of it to people who discuss it upon the political or the moral plane' (p. 58). This, Sartre explains, is why he employs the word 'humanism' to describe existentialism, and why he consents to the popularization of existentialism. The term 'humanism' indicates the refusal to restrict existentialism 'strictly to the philosophic plane and rely upon chance for any action upon it' (p. 58). It makes clear that existentialism is addressed to all human beings. Popularization is necessary so that the commitment existentialism demands can be understood and acted upon by all.

In response to the comment that only those who want to understand Sartre will understand him, Sartre argues that the questioner's observation expresses the outmoded view that philosophy interests only philosophers and not ordinary people, who are allegedly incapable of understanding it. But this is no longer the case, for the public 'have made philosophy come right down into the market-place' (p. 58). Sartre cites the example of Marx, who 'himself never ceased to popularise his thought' (p. 58), and points out that, 'The manifesto is the popularisation of an idea' (p. 58).

Sartre's mention of Marx elicits from the questioner the observation, 'The original choice of Marx was a revolutionary one' (p. 58). Sartre responds that since Marx was both a philosopher and a revolutionary, it is impossible to say which came first (pp. 58–9). The questioner replies with the claim that the *Communist Manifesto* is not a popularization, but a weapon of war, and that he 'cannot believe that it was not an act of commitment' (p. 59). The questioner goes on to point out that when Marx realized revolution was necessary, his first action was to write the *Communist Manifesto*. There is thus a clear connection between Marx's philosophy and political action. With Sartre, however, there is no such close logical connection between morality and philosophy.

Sartre counters this criticism by stating that existentialism is concerned with 'a morality of freedom', and that 'so long as there is no contradiction between that morality and our philosophy, nothing more is required' (p. 59). Furthermore, 'Types of commitment differ from one epoch to another' (p. 59). In an epoch in which commitment meant revolution it was appropriate for Marx to write the *Communist Manifesto*, but we no longer live in such an epoch. In the present age there exists a variety of parties, each claiming to be the party of revolution. In such circumstances, 'commitment does not consist in joining one of them, but in seeking to clarify the conception, in order to define the situation and at the same time to try to influence the different revolutionary practices' (p. 59).

The most important contribution to the discussion is made by the Marxist Pierre Naville, who gives a lengthy response to Sartre's lecture in which he raises some important points of criticism. Naville begins his response by claiming that Sartre's viewpoint raises the question whether his doctrine will not 'present itself, in the period now beginning, as the resurrection of radical-socialism?' (p. 59). Naville's point is not completely clear, but he seems to be accusing Sartre of wishing to return to a pre-Marxist and to Naville's mind now outmoded form of socialism. Naville admits that, 'This may seem fantastic, but it is the way in which one must now frame the question' (p. 59). Naville expands on these comments by claiming that Sartre seems to be offering 'a kind of resurrection of liberalism' (p. 60). According to Naville, Sartre's 'philosophy seeks to revive, in the quite peculiar conditions which are our present historical conditions, what is essential in radical-socialism, in liberal humanism' (p. 60). What distinguishes Sartre's version of liberal humanism from older liberalism is its emphasis on anguish, which is the result of the awareness that 'the social crisis of the world has gone too far for the old liberalism' (p. 60). As evidence for this view Naville cites Sartre's emphasis on 'the dignity of man, the eminent value of personality', which are themes that 'are not so far from those of the old liberalism' (p. 60). According to Naville, Sartre justifies his emphasis on human dignity and the value of personality by distinguishing 'between two meanings of "the condition of man" and between two meanings of several terms which are in common use' (p. 60). Naville decides to pass over the questions of philosophical technique which Sartre's invention of new meanings for equivocal terms raises and focuses instead on what he considers to be the 'fundamental point' which shows that despite Sartre's distinction between two meanings of humanism, he still adheres to the older meaning of the term (p. 60).

Naville summarizes Sartre's philosophy as the view that the human being 'presents himself as a choice to be made'. As Naville understands Sartre, this means the human being 'is, first and foremost, his existence at the present instant'. This in turn means that the human being 'stands outside of natural determinism', and is 'not defined by anything prior to himself, but by his present functioning as an individual'

(p. 60). Naville concludes his summary by noting that Sartre's philosophy claims 'there is no human nature superior' to the human being, 'but a specific existence is given to him at a given moment' (p. 60). The point on which Naville wishes to challenge Sartre is whether Sartre's concept of 'existence' is 'another form of the concept of human nature which, for historical reasons, is appearing in a novel guise' (p. 60). Naville claims that the eighteenth-century conception that Sartre repudiates reappears in Sartre's notion of 'the condition of man', which Naville sees as merely 'a substitute for human nature' (p. 60). Naville justifies this critique by attempting to show that Sartre's notion of human condition is tantamount to the affirmation of the concept of human nature. He claims: 'If we consider human conditions as conditions defined by X, which is the X of the subject, and not by the natural environment, not by positive determinants, one is considering human nature under another form' (p. 61). Naville describes this as 'a nature-condition'. Naville emphasizes that he does not mean by this term that the human being possesses 'an abstract type of nature', but means that for historical reasons human nature 'is revealed in ways much more difficult to formulate' (p. 61). The reason for the difficulty of defining human beings' 'nature-condition' is that the contemporary disintegration of social orders and social classes, and the 'stirring-together of all races and nations' (p. 61) means, 'The notion of a uniform and schematic human nature cannot now be presented with the same character of generality nor take on the same aspect of universality as in the eighteenth century, an epoch when it appeared to be definable upon a basis of continuous progress' (p. 61). Because we today no longer think in eighteenth-century terms, we have substituted the eighteenth-century notion 'with an expression of human nature which

both thoughtful and simple people call the condition of man'
(p. 61). People's presentation of this human condition, however, 'is vague, chaotic and generally of an aspect that is, so
to speak, dramatic; imposed by the circumstances' (p. 61).
Those who 'do not want to go beyond the general expression
of that condition into a deterministic enquiry into what the
effective conditions are', Naville claims, 'maintain the type
and scheme of an abstract expression, analogous to that of
human nature' (p. 61).

These comments apply to existentialism which, despite
Sartre's claims to the contrary, does indeed 'depend upon the
notion of the nature of man, but this time it is not a nature
that has pride in itself, but one that is fearful, uncertain and
forlorn' (p. 61). Naville expands on this claim by considering
in more detail what existentialism means by 'human condition'. As used by the existentialist, the phrase 'human condition', Naville claims, refers to a 'pre-condition' in which the
human being 'is not yet really committed to what existentialism calls purposes' (p. 61). Consequently, what the existentialist is speaking of is 'a pre-engagement, not a commitment, not
even a real condition' (p. 61). This explains why the human
condition 'is defined primarily by its general, humanist character' (p. 61). In the past 'human nature' denoted 'something
more limited than if one were speaking of a condition in general', for 'Human nature is not a modality in the sense that the
condition of man is a modality' (p. 61). Naville's point seems to
be that the term 'condition' is broader than that of 'nature', for
it describes not merely *what* but *how* the human being is. This
prompts Naville to suggest that it would be more appropriate
'to speak of naturalism than of humanism', because 'naturalism' implies realities more general than are implied in Sartre's
use of the term 'humanism'. For Naville, when we employ the

term 'naturalism', 'we are dealing with reality itself' (p. 62). Naville goes on to make the further point that the discussion of human nature 'needs to be widened: for the historical point of view must also be considered' (p. 62). For Naville, 'The primary reality is that of nature, of which human reality is only one function' (p. 62). But if this is the case, then 'one must admit the truth of history' (p. 62), something which according to Naville the existentialist refuses to do. History, Naville claims, is what makes human beings individuals. It is, he claims, because of human beings' 'actual history' that human beings never live 'in a world which provides an abstract condition for them' (p. 62). It is because human beings have a history that we can speak of the human condition. As Naville puts it, 'Because of their history they appear in a world of which they themselves have always been part and parcel, by which they are conditioned and to the conditions of which they contribute, even as the mother conditions her child and the child also conditions her from the beginning of its gestation' (p. 62). It is only in this sense that it is valid 'to speak of the condition of man as of a primary reality' (p. 62). But this means, Naville claims, 'One ought rather to say that the primary reality is a natural condition and not a human condition' (p. 62). Naville fails to see how existentialism is able to refute these 'current and common opinions' he has outlined, and points out that just as there can be no abstract human nature or essence that precedes the human being's existence, so too can there be no human condition in general. This applies even if Sartre 'mean[s] by condition a certain set of concrete circumstances or situations', for Sartre fails to articulate what these are. The Marxist view is in any case different, for it affirms 'nature within man and man within nature, which is not necessarily defined from an individual point of view' (p. 62).

These considerations lead Naville to claim 'that there are laws of the functioning of man, as of every object of science, which constitute, in the full sense of the word, his nature' (p. 62). While Naville is prepared to concede that this human nature is variable, he claims that this notion of human nature 'bears little resemblance to a **phenomenology** – that is, to any perception of it that is felt, empirical, or lived, or such as is given by common sense or rather by the assumed common sense of the philosophers' (p. 62). Consequently, the eighteenth-century conception of nature 'was undoubtedly much nearer to that of Marx than is its existentialist substitute, "the condition of man" – which is a pure phenomenology of his situation' (p. 62).

Naville's next point concerns the meaning of 'humanism'. This term, he points out, has been used to identify many different philosophical tendencies. 'We are', he claims , 'all humanists to-day' (p. 63). Marxists, classical rationalists, Christianity, Hinduism, and other religions, existentialists, indeed, all philosophers, as well as many political movements, all claim to be humanist. For Naville, all these various claims to the title of 'humanism' are 'a kind of attempt to re-instate a philosophy which, for all its claims, refuses in the last resort to commit itself, not only from the political or social standpoint, but also in the deeper philosophic sense' (p. 63). As examples of humanism as a failure of commitment Naville cites Christianity and 'the pseudo-Marxists or the liberals'. Christianity's claim to be humanist expresses merely its inability to detach itself from reactionary positions and commit itself to the progressive forces working for the revolution. Similarly, the pseudo-Marxist or liberal emphasis on the primacy of the rights of the individual 'is because they recoil before the exigencies of the present world situation' (p. 63).

The same applies to the existentialist who, 'like the liberal, puts in a claim for man in general because he cannot manage to formulate such a position as the events require' (p. 63). For Naville the 'only progressive position' is Marxism, for 'Marxism alone states the real problems of the age' (p. 63).

Naville now turns to criticize the existentialist notion of freedom. 'It is not true', he claims, 'that a man has freedom of choice, in the sense that by that choice he confers upon his activity a meaning it would not otherwise have' (p. 63). Naville cites two reasons for this. First, 'It is not enough to say that men can strive for freedom without knowing that they strive for it' (p. 63). Second, and following on from this, it is clearly the case that human beings 'can engage in the struggle for a cause which over-rules them'. This indicates that human beings 'can act within a frame greater than themselves, and not merely act out of themselves' (p. 63). Furthermore, to state that the human being strives for freedom but without stating how or for what goal he is striving is to state that that individual's actions create 'a succession of consequences weaving themselves into a whole network of causality of which he cannot grasp all the effects, but which, all the same, round off his action and endow it with a meaning, in function with the activity of others' (p. 63). For Sartre, however, 'the choice is a pre-choice' (p. 64), which Naville takes to indicate a concern with 'the freedom of a prior indifference' (p. 64).

Sartre's notions of human condition and freedom, Naville continues, are dependent upon 'a certain definition of the objective', namely upon the 'idea of the world of objects as utilities' (p. 64). According to Naville, Sartre has imposed 'an image of beings existing in discontinuity' on to the world of objects, thereby creating 'a picture of a discontinuous world of objects, in which there is no causality, excepting that strange variety of causal relatedness which is that of utility – passive, incomprehensible and contemptible' (p. 64). For Naville existentialism is characterized by an 'implemental mode of determinism' according to which the world is full of 'untidy obstacles, entangled and piled up one upon another in a fantastic desire to make them serve one another, but all branded with the stigma, so frightful in the eyes of idealists, of their so-called pure exteriority' (p. 64). Such an understanding of the world is 'a-causal', 'wholly arbitrary and in no way agrees with the data of modern science' (p. 64). This a-causal arbitrary conception of the world stems from the existentialist separation of the world from the human condition, a separation which for Naville makes the world of objects described by existentialism unreal. For Naville, the world is an entirety encompassing both human beings and objects. Consequently, 'the whole of this world . . . may be seen, in certain variable conditions, under the sign of **objectivity**' (p. 64). Naville refuses to be drawn into arguments about the utility 'of stars, of anger, of a flower' (p. 64), and maintains that Sartre's freedom, which Naville categorizes as **idealism**, 'is made out of an arbitrary contempt for things' (p. 64). To this criticism Naville adds the further objection that things are very different from the way Sartre describes them. Although Sartre recognizes the existence of things in their own right, he views the existence of the objective world in negative terms, namely as a relationship of 'permanent hostility' to human beings. For Sartre the objective universe 'is never . . . a condition or a source of conditioning' but is only 'an occasion of vexation, a thing elusive, fundamentally indifferent, a continual mere probability' (p. 64). The existentialist view of the universe is thus 'the very opposite of what it is to the Marxist materialist' (p. 64).

Because of such views Sartre 'can only conceive the commitment of philosophy as an arbitrary decision which you describe as free' (pp. 64–5). Naville accuses Sartre of denaturing history. As an example he cites Sartre's view of Marx. Sartre claims that Marx 'has outlined a philosophy because he was committed to it' (p. 65). But for Naville, Marx 'distilled' his philosophy 'out of a multiplicity of experiences'. As evidence for this, Naville points out that 'the development of philosophic thinking in Marx took place in conscious connection with the development of politics and society' (p. 65). Marx is not unique in this respect, for the thinking of earlier philosophers also took place in relation to political and social factors. This is the case even with philosophers who did not get involved in political activity such as Kant and Descartes, for even their philosophies had a political dimension. Naville describes Sartre's attempts 'to re-establish, in any form whatsoever, a position anterior to Marxism' as 'going back to radical-socialism' (p. 65).

Naville calls upon existentialism to 'undertake first of all a work of self-criticism' if it is to engender a will to revolution (p. 65). This will require those who advocate existentialism to undergo a 'dialectical crisis', if existentialism is 'to retain, in some sense, certain positions not devoid of value which are held by some of its partisans' (p. 65). This is made all the more necessary by the fact that some adherents of existentialism 'have been arguing from existentialism to social conclusions that are most disquieting, indeed obviously retrograde' (p. 65). As an example Naville cites an unnamed individual who claimed that phenomenology could provide 'the *petite*-bourgeoisie with a philosophy which would enable them to live and to become the vanguard of the international revolutionary movement' (p. 65). This is just one example of many others that could be cited of people who are drawn to existentialism and use it as the basis for developing political theories. Such theories, Naville claims, are 'coloured with neo-liberalism, with neo-radical-socialism', which Naville sees as a danger (p. 66). What chiefly interests Naville is the orientation of the themes of existentialism, for these themes 'do lead to something', even when existentialists are perhaps unaware of this. He concedes that existentialism does not lead to quietism but argues that it fosters 'something very like "attentism"', i.e. an attitude of not committing oneself until it has become clear which is the winning side. Although this attitude may be consistent with certain types of individual commitment, it is not compatible 'with any search for a commitment of collective value – especially of a prescriptive value' (p. 66). 'Why', Naville asks, 'should existentialism not give any directions?' (p. 66). Naville ends his lengthy response by stating that existentialism 'ought to give directives'. In 1945, the year of Sartre's lecture, existentialism ought to tell us which political party we should join and 'whether it is on the side of the workers or on that of the *petite*-bourgeoisie' (p. 66).

Sartre begins his response by voicing his opinion that Naville has taken up 'a dogmatic position' (p. 66). Naville has claimed that existentialism adopts 'a position anterior to Marxism', but for Sartre what Naville must prove 'is that the position we are seeking to establish is not post-Marxian' (p. 66). Sartre, however, does not pursue this point but turns to Naville's conception of truth. Naville, Sartre points out, 'think[s] there are some things that are absolutely true, for you present your objections in the name of a certitude' (p. 66). Sartre asks how Naville has arrived at such certitude if, as one of his objections to Sartre's lecture has indicated, he views all human beings as objects. Furthermore, Naville is mistaken in his claim that 'it is in the name of human dignity that man refuses to regard man as an object' (p. 66). The refusal to regard the human being as an object 'is for a reason of a philosophic and logical order' (pp. 66–7), namely that, 'if you postulate a universe of objects, truth disappears' (p. 67). This, Sartre claims, is because 'the objective world is the world of the probable' and therefore Naville 'ought to recognise that every theory, whether scientific or philosophic, is one of probability' (p. 67). As evidence for the validity of his claim Sartre points to the fact that 'scientific and historical theses vary, and that they are made in the form of hypotheses' (p. 67). The fact that the objective world is a world of probabilities raises the question about the source of our certitude. This question, Sartre claims, can be better answered on existentialist terms than from the position Naville has adopted, for 'our subjectivism allows us some certitudes'. Consequently, Sartre is in a position to justify the dogmatism Naville has demonstrated in his discourse, but Naville's dogmatism 'is incomprehensible from the position' that Naville himself takes (p. 67). And, Sartre asks, if Naville is unable to define the truth, how can he be sure that Marxism 'has no more than theoretical value?' (p. 67). Also, 'How can one make a dialectic of history unless one begins by postulating a certain number of rules?' (p. 67). Existentialism is able to answer such questions by deducing rules 'from the Cartesian *cogito*', which allows us to find answers 'by placing ourselves firmly upon the ground of subjectivity' (p. 67). Sartre emphasizes he is not disputing 'the fact that, continually, man is an object to man', but this fact must be supplemented by the awareness that 'in order to grasp the object as it is, there must be a subject which attains to itself as subject' (p. 67).

Sartre then turns to Naville's comments concerning the human condition, noting that Naville sometimes describes it as 'a pre-condition' but also speaks of 'pre-determination'. Naville's comments reveal he has failed to realize that Sartre accepts 'much that is in the Marxian descriptions' (p. 67). It is also wrong to criticize Sartre on the same grounds on which Naville criticizes the thinkers of the eighteenth century, 'who were ignorant of the whole question' (p. 67). Naville's comments about determinism are well known to existentialism, for which 'the real problem is to define conditions in which there can be universality' (p. 67). The problem, as Sartre understands it, is that, 'Since there is no human nature, how can one preserve, throughout the continual changes of history, universal principles sufficient to interpret, for instance, the phenomenon of Spartacus, which presupposes a minimum understanding of that epoch?' (p. 67). Sartre holds that he and Naville are in agreement in holding 'there is no human nature; in other words, each epoch develops according to dialectical laws, and men depend upon their epoch and not upon human nature' (p. 67).

Naville responds by commenting that when we discuss a past epoch we do so by considering 'what is analogous or different in the social life of that epoch compared with that of our own' (p. 68). If, however, 'we tried to analyse the analogy itself as a function of some abstract kind, we should never arrive at anything' (p. 68). We would no longer have a yardstick by which we could compare the present with the past. Naville takes Sartre to be arguing that, 'after two thousand years, one has no means of analysing the present situation except certain observations upon the condition of man in general' (p. 68). This would mean, Naville claims, that it would be impossible to conduct a retrospective analysis.

Sartre denies he has ever doubted 'the need for analysis either of human conditions or of individual intentions' (p. 68).

He clarifies what he means by 'situation' by describing it as 'the whole of the conditions, not only material but psycho-analytic, which, in the epoch under consideration, define it precisely as a whole' (p. 68). If this is the case, Naville argues, then Sartre's definition is not in conformity with his writings. It is in any case clear that Sartre's conception of the situation differs fundamentally from that of Marxism, 'in that it denies causality' (p. 68). Sartre's definition is imprecise, slides between different positions, and is insufficiently rigorous. The Marxist view, on the other hand, is that 'a situation is a totality that is constructed, and that reveals itself, by a whole series of determining factors, and these determinants are causal, including causality of a statistical kind' (p. 68).

Sartre holds that Naville's notion of 'causality of a statistical order' is 'meaningless', and asks Naville to provide a precise and clear definition of causality. For Naville to respond to the concept of freedom by stating, 'Excuse me, but there is causality', is of no help, for he is unable to render an account of 'this secret causality' (p. 68). Naville, Sartre comments, has 'a dream about the Marxian causality' (p. 69).

Naville responds by asking Sartre whether he admits the existence of scientific truth. Although 'there may be spheres in which no kind of truth is predicable', Sartre must surely concede that the world of objects 'is the world with which the sciences are concerned' (p. 69). If Sartre holds that 'this is a world in which there are only probabilities, never amounting to the truth', then this means that the world of objects which is the concern of science can never achieve absolute truth but only relative truth. Naville asks Sartre whether he 'will admit that the sciences employ the notion of causality' (p. 69).

Sartre is not prepared to accept Naville's request on the grounds that 'the sciences are abstract; they study the variations of factors that are equally abstract, and not real causality' (p. 69). Sartre, on the other hand, is 'concerned with universal factors upon a plane where their relations can always be studied'. In Marxism, however, 'one is engaged in the study of a single totality, in which one searches for causality' (p. 69). This Marxist notion of causality, Sartre points out, 'is not at all the same thing as scientific causality' (p. 69).

Naville turns to Sartre's example of the young man who came to Sartre for advice. If Naville had been in Sartre's position he 'would have endeavoured to ascertain what were [the young man's] capabilities, his age, his financial resources; and to look into his relation to his mother' (p. 69). On this basis Naville would 'most certainly have tried to arrive at a definite point of view', even if his advice might prove wrong when acted upon. In contrast to Sartre, however, Naville would have recommended to the young man a definite course of action.

Sartre responds by repeating the point he made in the lecture that the young man has already chosen the answer to his question in choosing his adviser. Sartre admits he would have been capable of giving the young man practical advice, 'but as he was seeking freedom I wanted to let him decide' (p. 70). Sartre concludes his answer and the discussion with the comment that he in any case knew what the young man was going to do, and that the young man did indeed do what Sartre expected him to do.

Detailed Summary of Existentialism and Humanism

Overview

The Critique of Existentialism (pp. 23–6)

Existentialism has been accused of being an individualistic bourgeois philosophy of quietism and despair that teaches there are no solutions to human beings' problems and that therefore all our actions in this world are ineffectual. A further criticism is that existentialism emphasizes what is ignominious in the human situation and completely ignores the brighter side of human nature. The Communists allege that the dependence of existentialism on the notion of pure subjectivity derived from Descartes' *cogito ergo sum* undermines human solidarity, while Christians criticize existentialism for ignoring the commandments of God and rejecting eternal values. The Christians further claim that because existentialism allegedly teaches 'everybody can do what he likes', existentialism is unable to distinguish between right and wrong. *Existentialism and Humanism* is a reply to these criticisms.

The 'essential charge' levelled at existentialism is that it overemphasizes 'the evil side of human life'. It is puzzling that people are scandalized and horrified by existentialism, since more cynical views of human beings can be found in popular proverbs such as 'Charity begins at home' and 'Promote a rogue and he'll sue you for damage, knock him down and he'll do you homage'. The excessive protests of people against existentialism indicate that it is not the pessimism but rather the *optimism* of existentialism that alarms them. This optimism stems from the fact that existentialism confronts human beings with the possibility of *choice*.

Understanding what existentialism is has been hampered by the fact that the term has been misunderstood and misused. Existentialism has become a fad and has been seized upon by people who are eager to join in the latest scandal or movement, but who have little knowledge of the real meaning of existentialism. The situation is complicated still further by the fact that there are *two* types of existentialism, namely, Christian existentialism and atheistic existentialism. What unites both types is their common commitment to the principle that *existence precedes essence*, or, to put it another way, that philosophy must take the human subject as its starting-point.

Existence Precedes Essence (pp. 26–8)

To clarify the meaning of *existence precedes essence*, Sartre compares the existence of the human being with the existence of an article of manufacture such as a book or a paper-knife. The artisan makes a paper-knife according to a certain plan and by means of certain methods of production. If we express this in philosophical terms, we can say that the *essence* of the paper-knife, i.e. the idea of the paper-knife that the artisan must have in mind in order to make the paper-knife, *precedes* its *existence*.

The principle that 'essence precedes existence' has been applied by religious believers to human beings. When we conceive of God as creator, we conceive of him as 'a supernal artisan'. Like the artisan making a paper-knife, God creates human beings according to a plan, and each human being is the realization of a conception which resides in the divine understanding. Even when the notion of God is suppressed, the priority of essence over existence persists in the belief that human beings possess a common human nature. Kant provides a good example of this belief in a universal human nature, for he holds that the wild man of the woods, i.e. the human being in the state of nature, and the bourgeois individual both share the same fundamental qualities.

Atheistic existentialism rejects the existence of God, but holds that there is nevertheless one being whose existence precedes its essence. This is the human being. It is not a God-given blueprint or a fixed, universal human nature, but the *individual human being* who decides what he or she will be. The human being is what he wills, and his conception of what he is comes *after* he has willed to become what he is. This is the 'first principle of existentialism', namely that the human being is what he makes of himself.

Subjectivity and Responsibility (pp. 28–30)

Those who reproach existentialism with 'subjectivity' fail to realize that this first principle of existentialism means that the human being is of a greater dignity than a stone or a table. *Existence precedes essence* means that in contrast to other things in the world the human being is a 'project', i.e. a being which propels itself towards a future and is aware of doing so. The human being exists only through will and decision.

The existentialist understanding of 'will' and 'decision' should not be confused with the common view of the will as a conscious decision taken after we have made ourselves what we are, such as joining a political party, writing a book, or getting married. These are only manifestations of a prior, more fundamental act of will. Existentialism is concerned with this more fundamental act of will by means of which the human being creates him or herself.

There is thus a close connection between the principle of 'existence precedes essence' and *responsibility*. This is not merely individual responsibility, however, but responsibility for all human beings. When a human being chooses himself, he simultaneously chooses for *all* human beings. This is because when choosing himself the human being is choosing an image of what he believes *all* human beings ought to be. Consequently, in choosing ourselves we are taking responsibility for all human beings, for in fashioning our own individual image through this choice, we assume that this image is valid for all our contemporaries. To illustrate the connection between choice and responsibility Sartre cites the choices of joining a trade union and getting married. If a person decides to join a Christian rather than a communist trade union, he or she is affirming the view that resignation rather than political resistance is the appropriate form of existence for human beings. Similarly, if a person marries, he or she is implicitly affirming the validity of monogamy for all human beings. In choosing for myself, I unavoidably choose for others, and consequently I am responsible not only for myself but for all human beings.

Anguish (pp. 30–2)

It is the emphasis on the responsibility of choice that accounts for the existentialist notions of anguish, abandonment and despair. The burden of responsibility of choosing on behalf of all humankind is the cause of anguish to the human being.

People who choose without any apparent sign of anguish are either disguising or fleeing from their anguish. The person who is unconcerned at the implication of his or her choice for other human beings is guilty of *bad faith*, for one ought always to ask oneself what would happen if everyone did as one is doing. Furthermore, such an individual reveals his anguish by his attempts to disguise it, for when he lies in self-excuse, by stating his conviction that not everyone will carry out the actions he has chosen for himself, he has assumed the universal validity of the value from which he wishes to exempt himself.

To illustrate the nature of anguish Sartre takes Kierkegaard's example of Abraham's anguish when commanded by an angel to sacrifice his son. Abraham's anguish comes from *his* choice to sacrifice Isaac. It was his choice, because he *chose* to understand the angel's words as a divine command. Another example of the anguish of choice is provided by a woman who claims she is receiving divine orders through the telephone. The decision to understand these phone calls to come from God is *her* decision. In such decisions there is no objective proof or sign to prove beyond doubt that the individual is making the *right* decision. The responsibility lies wholly with the individual. It is this responsibility and the individual's knowledge that when making his/her choice it is as if the whole human race were watching and regulating itself by that individual's behaviour that is the cause of anguish. Any human being who does not ask himself whether his choice of action is one that all human beings should follow is refusing to face up to his anguish.

This anguish does not paralyse the individual into inactivity, however. On the contrary, anguish is the condition of action, for anguish is the recognition of the range of possibilities open to the human being and the responsibility the human being must take in choosing one of these possibilities. It is with this type of anguish, i.e. with anguish as a condition of action, with which existentialism is concerned.

Overview

Abandonment (pp. 32-9)

By 'abandonment' existentialists mean that human beings must follow through to their logical conclusion the consequences of the non-existence of God. Sartre criticizes late nineteenth-century French atheists for attempting to find an *a priori*, objective basis in the intelligibility of the world for the moral values of honesty, progress and humanity. Their rejection of God thus changed nothing, for they continued to believe in objective moral values, the only difference being that the source of these values was found not in God but in a non-religious objective source. For the existentialist, however, the non-existence of God removes not only the religious basis of moral values but undermines *all* attempts to ground morality on an objective foundation. It is this loss of objective foundations that existentialism takes as its starting-point. If there is no God, the human being is 'abandoned' because there is nothing outside of himself to give him guidance. Consequently, the human being alone must take responsibility for himself, for it is he alone who decides his actions. For human beings living in a Godless universe existence precedes essence, which means human beings cannot appeal to a given and specific human nature to justify their actions. This means there is no determinism, for the human being can never appeal to external factors to justify his or her actions. Each human being is free, indeed, the human being *is* freedom. Sartre describes the human being as being 'condemned' to be free, because although he did not create himself, as a free being he is nevertheless responsible for everything he does. The human being cannot even appeal to passion, for to claim that one has been swept away by a grand passion is to refuse to face up to one's responsibility for one's passion. Nor can the human being appeal to some sign to guide his actions, for each human being is responsible for the way he interprets the sign he takes to guide him. The human being is on his own and he alone must decide how he will act, and he alone must take responsibility for that decision. The human being is condemned at every instant to invent himself.

To illustrate his point Sartre cites the example of a young man who sought his advice on whether he should stay with his mother or join the French resistance. This young man was confronted by the choice between a concrete, immediate action for the benefit of a single individual and an action in the service of a collectivity which he might be unable to bring to completion. The young man was also confronted by the choice between, on the one hand, 'the morality of sympathy' and 'personal devotion' and, on the other hand, a wider morality that was of more debatable validity. There is no authoritative source of guidance to which he can turn to help him resolve this dilemma. Christianity merely preaches a doctrine of charity, love of neighbour, self-denial, and choosing the hardest way, but it provides no guidance on *what* is the hardest way. It is thus unable to help the young man to decide between the two choices confronting him. Nor does Kantianism provide any guidance. The Kantian ethic that we should never regard another human being as a means, but always as an end applies to both the choices facing the young man. If he chooses to stay with his mother he will be treating her as an end and not as a means, but he will then be treating as a means those who are fighting to liberate France on his behalf. But if the young man abandons his mother and joins the French resistance, then he will be treating his comrades in the resistance as the end and his mother merely as a means.

One way of resolving this dilemma might be to trust one's

feelings or instincts. Thus the young man could ask himself whether his loyalty to his mother or his desire to join the resistance was stronger. Whichever feeling was stronger would be the guide to his decision on how to act. The problem with this solution is that the strength of our feelings is proved by our *acting* on those feelings. But if I prove the strength of my feeling by acting upon it, then I have *already* chosen my course of action. This is a vicious circle in which feeling justifies action, and action justifies the feeling which prompted action.

There is a further problem in using one's feelings to justify a decision, namely the difficulty of distinguishing between real feelings and play-acting. Whether one is play-acting or genuinely acting in response to one's feelings can be decided only by acting on one's feelings. But this again means that action becomes the guide to the genuineness of feeling, thereby undermining the attempt to make feeling the guide of action. Feeling, then, is of no assistance in helping us to decide between two rival courses of action.

The fact that the young man asked a professor for advice does not refute Sartre's argument that there can be no objective guidance to help us in our choice of actions, for the young man's choice of adviser shows he has already decided on his course of action. For example, if a Christian consults a priest for guidance, his choice of a priest who is on the side of the resistance or is a collaborator with the Nazis shows he has already chosen his course of action before he receives the priest's advice. In coming to an existentialist philosopher for guidance, the young man knew exactly what sort of advice he was going to receive, namely that there is no rule of general morality to guide him and that he is free and therefore must choose and invent himself.

If the Catholic objects that there are indeed signs which can guide us in our actions, then all that this shows is again that the Catholic objector has already made his choice. There is nothing in the 'signs' themselves that can give us guidance, for the Catholic's interpretation of the signs as signs is due to his or her choice. Thus it is the Jesuit priest's *decision* to interpret his unhappy childhood and unsuccessful adolescence as a divine sign that he should devote his life to religion. Others could have interpreted these setbacks quite differently and have become something quite different from a Jesuit priest, such as, for example, a carpenter or a revolutionary. It is the Jesuit's decision to interpret the events of his life as signs of a divine calling, and he alone bears the responsibility for this decision.

'Abandonment' thus means that each of us decides our being with no guidance to help us, which is why abandonment is always accompanied by anguish.

Despair (pp. 39–44)

'Despair' means living within one's possibilities and acting on those possibilities, a point made by Descartes when he said, 'Conquer yourself rather than the world', which according to Sartre means human beings should act without hope. The limitation of oneself to the possibilities contained in one's will, and the call to conquer oneself rather than the world are 'despair' because they require us to give up hope in another power to shape our lives for us. We are in despair, because there is nothing in which we can hope.

To this the Marxist might object that although the individual's action is ultimately limited by his or her death, each human being can rely on the help of others to continue the struggle for the revolution. Sartre responds to this objection by arguing that relying on one's comrades is like relying on the train to arrive on time or the tram not to be derailed when waiting for the arrival of a friend. That is, the action of my comrades belongs to the probabilities of my life which I take into consideration when deciding on my own actions. But because the human being is free and there is no fixed human nature to which I can appeal, I cannot rely on human beings to continue my work. The impossibility of guaranteeing that my actions will be continued by others should not prompt me to give up, however. On the contrary, I should continue to commit myself and act on my commitments, but I should do so without illusion. The success or failure of my ventures does not lie in my hands, but it is my task to do what I can.

Existentialism thus in no way supports quietism, which is the attitude of people who sit back and let others act. Existentialism calls upon human beings to act without regard for the success or failure of their actions. The precept of existentialism is that the human being is the sum of his or her actions. This is why some people are horrified by existentialism. Because action is what makes the human being what he or she is, existentialism confronts human beings starkly with their responsibility for their lives. There are no excuses. Only action is reality, and everything else – dreams, expectations and hopes – is delusion. Existentialism teaches that the human being is the sum of the actions he or she chooses to take.

When people accuse existentialism of pessimism they are really criticizing the sternness of existentialism's optimism. For example, people condemn existentialist novels because the characters' baseness, weakness and cowardice are attributed not to such external factors as heredity or environment, but solely to the characters themselves. The coward, for example, is not a coward because of his physiological make-up or because he has a cowardly temperament, but because he has *chosen* to make himself into a coward by his actions. It is existentialism's attribution of responsibility to the individual that people find so disturbing. They would prefer to be born either a coward or a hero, because they could then absolve themselves of responsibility for their actions with the argument that they were simply following their given nature. The existentialist rejects this view as a denial of responsibility and openly confronts the individual with his responsibility for his actions.

The reproaches made against existentialism are thus mistaken. Existentialism is not a philosophy of quietism, nor is it pessimistic, nor does it discourage human beings from action. Existentialism is an ethic of action and self-commitment.

Inter-Subjectivity (pp. 44–6)

Existentialism has been accused of confining the human being within his or her individual subjectivity. But existentialists take subjectivity as their point of departure because, as Descartes' *cogito ergo sum* ('I think, therefore I am') makes clear, our immediate sense of our own selves is the only truth of which we can be absolutely certain. Furthermore, existentialism is the only philosophy that does justice to human dignity, for it is the only philosophy which does not reduce human beings to objects. Existentialism should not be understood as narrowly individual subjectivism, for it is not only one's own self that one discovers in the immediate sense of one's own existence, but also the selves of other people. This is because the human being knows him or herself not as an isolated self but as a self in relation to other selves, and because other human beings play a vital role in the self-knowledge of each individual human being. For example, a human being cannot recognize himself as spiritual, wicked, or jealous, unless he is recognized as such by other human beings. This discovery of myself through my relationship with others is simultaneously the revelation of the other as a freedom which confronts mine. This means that human beings live in a world characterized by 'inter-subjectivity'. It is in relationship with others in this world of inter-subjectivity that each individual has to decide what he or she is.

The Human Condition (pp. 46–7)

Although there is no such thing as a universal human nature, there is a human universality of condition, which consists of the *limitations* which define the situation in which human beings find themselves. Thus regardless of whether a person is born a slave, feudal baron or proletarian, he or she will be confronted by the necessities of being in the world, of having to labour and to die there. These limitations of human existence are both subjective and objective. They are objective because we confront them and recognize them everywhere. They are subjective because every individual human being must choose how to shape his or her existence in relation to these limitations. A further indication of a universal human condition is that no human purpose is wholly foreign or incomprehensible to other human beings. This human universality of condition, however, is not something which is objectively given, but is being perpetually made and remade by human beings. No purpose defines a human being for ever, for a human being can always decide to choose himself anew. What is universal is the task of choosing oneself within the limitations imposed by the situation into which each human being is born.

Commitment, Choice and Bad Faith (pp. 47–54)

Central to existentialism is the absolute character of the human being's free commitment. It is through this free commitment that every human being realizes him or herself, and in doing so realizes a type of humanity in the world. It is only this *commitment* that is absolute, not the cultural forms which human beings' commitment creates, which are always only relative. Consequently, there is no difference between free being and absolute being. Free being is self-commitment. It is existence choosing its essence through self-commitment. Free being is thus also absolute being, because self-commitment is absolute to all human beings. There is also no difference between absolute being, which manifests itself in the temporally and historically localized forms chosen by human beings, and universally intelligible being, for every human being recognizes and understands the absoluteness of commitment, even though the types of humanity that result from this commitment are culturally and historically conditioned.

This argument, however, does not completely refute the charge of subjectivism, as can be seen from the fact that the charge reappears in new guises. Existentialism is accused, first, of teaching that 'it does not matter what you do'; second, of having no standards by which it would be possible to judge others; and third, of holding that everything is voluntary. None of these criticisms should be taken seriously. The objection that it does not matter what one chooses, fails to recognize the seriousness of choice, namely that it is impossible *not to choose*. Even choosing not to choose is a choice. Choosing is not capricious, for it takes place in a real situation. For example, the fact I am a sexual being capable of producing children compels me to choose my attitude to this situation. And in choosing one attitude over another I am choosing for all humankind, for I am implicitly affirming my conviction that this is the way *all* human beings should act. It is because in choosing for myself I am choosing for all human beings that my choice is not arbitrary or capricious but responsible.

There is thus a fundamental difference between the existentialist notion of choice and Gide's theory of the gratuitous act, which is a failure to recognize that human beings always choose *in a situation*. The existentialist recognizes that the human being is always involved in a situation and cannot avoid choosing for himself and thus for the whole of humankind in this situation. Existentialism's insistence that human beings choose in a situation means that although existentialism holds that the human being chooses without reference to any pre-established values, it is not advocating arbitrary choice.

The nature of existential choice is best understood when we compare it with a work of art. No one reproaches an artist for not painting a picture according to *a priori* rules, nor do we define in advance what picture he should paint. It is the artist who decides what and how he will paint. Despite the absence of *a priori* values, however, values are nevertheless present in the work of art's coherence and in the relation between the will to create and the finished work. Like art, morality is a creative and inventive act, for we cannot decide *a priori* what it is that should be done. This is clear from the example of the young man deciding whether he should stay with his mother or join the resistance. Because he was unable to find any guidance, he was compelled to invent the law for himself. Yet in neither course of action open to him could we accuse him of choosing moral irresponsibility. This example shows that the human being is not found ready-made but makes himself by the choice of his morality. And the human being cannot avoid this self-creative choice of morality, for he constantly lives in a situation that demands that he choose. To accuse existentialism of irresponsibility is thus simply absurd.

The second objection levelled against existentialism is that it is impossible to judge others on existentialist principles. This is both true and false. It is true because whatever choice a person makes it is impossible to prefer another for him. It is also true, because existentialists do not believe in progress, but believe that human beings always remain the same. Existentialists hold that although individual situations may change, human beings and the task of making a choice in a situation do not change. The critic of existentialism is thus in one sense right in claiming that existentialism makes it impossible to judge others. From the existentialist perspective it is impossible to pass judgement on others because the values of other people are the result of their own free decisions and are not justifiable by any objective criteria. In another sense, however, the critic is wrong, for it is indeed possible to judge others from the perspective of existentialism. Judgement of others is possible because in choosing himself the human being chooses in the view of other human beings. This means it is possible to make a *logical* judgement whether an individual's choice is founded upon an error or upon the truth. Thus it is possible to judge someone as guilty of bad faith if that person refuses to take responsibility for the choices he or she has freely made. But why should a person not choose bad faith, if this is the choice he or she has chosen to make? The existentialist's response is that such a person is guilty of inconsistency. The person of bad faith acknowledges neither his freedom nor his choice, but claims that the values he has in reality freely chosen for himself were imposed upon him. To act freely and yet to deny that freedom is inconsistent and self-contradictory, and can thus be condemned as a logical error.

Another way the existentialist can judge the person of bad faith is to pass a moral judgement. This moral judgement stems from the fact that freedom is an end in itself. Because he accepts that he himself must freely choose his values, the person of good faith recognizes that freedom is the foundation of all values. Consequently, the actions of people of good faith have as their aim freedom as such. The existentialist's aim is to will freedom for freedom's sake, not in an abstract sense but in particular circumstances. This does not isolate us from other human beings, however, because my freedom and the freedom of others are intimately connected. This stems from the concrete nature of freedom. When I understand freedom as an act of commitment in a particular, concrete situation, then I am obliged to will the liberty of others at the same time as I will mine. That is, because when I choose, I choose what I believe to be the right choice for *all* human beings, I cannot make freedom my aim unless I make the freedom of other human beings equally my aim.

It is this recognition of the primacy of freedom that enables me to pass judgement on the person of bad faith. Such judgement is undertaken in the name of that will to freedom which is implied in freedom itself. For the sake of freedom, the existentialist judges those who seek to flee from their freedom. Those who hide from their freedom by appealing to determinism are 'cowards', while those who claim that their existence is necessary when in fact it is merely an accident of the appearance of the human race on earth are 'scum'. 'Cowards' and 'scum' can be identified only 'upon the plane of strict authenticity'. Although the content of morality is variable, a certain form of morality is universal. Kant was right in declaring 'freedom is a will both to itself and to the freedom of others', but his abstract treatment of freedom is an insufficient basis for morality. The young man struggling to decide whether to stay with his mother or join the resistance illustrates the problem. There are no authoritative moral criteria that can help the young man with his decision. The content of the decision has always to be invented; that is, the individual decides not according to some abstract principle but always within the confines of the concrete situation in which he finds himself. We cannot judge the validity of the content of the decision, but we can judge whether another person's invention of his morality is made in the name of freedom.

Sartre cites the examples of Maggie Tulliver in George Eliot's *Mill on the Floss* and La Sanseverina in Stendhal's *Chartreuse de Parme* to illustrate this point. Maggie Tulliver decides in the name of human solidarity to sacrifice herself and to give up the man she loves. La Sanseverina on the other hand, Sartre claims, would choose in the name of passion to sacrifice not her own happiness but that of her rival. Despite their differences the two apparently opposite moralities of the two women are equivalent, for both have acted on their freedom. This shows that the objection that it is impossible for the existentialist to judge others is both true and false. The examples of Maggie Tulliver and La Sanseverina show that 'One can choose anything, but only if it is upon the plane of free commitment'.

The third objection to existentialism, namely that everything is voluntary, amounts to the accusation that the existentialist's values are not serious, because the existentialist chooses them himself. The only reply that can be made to this charge is that if there is no God, then human beings have to choose their own values. To accept that human beings must invent their values is to affirm that life has no *a priori* meaning. It is the human being who through his choices gives his life meaning and value.

Overview

Existentialism is a Humanism (pp. 54–6)

Some critics have challenged Sartre's claim that existentialism is a humanism and, furthermore, have accused Sartre
of inconsistency, since he has included a critique of humanism in his novel *Nausea*. This criticism is based, however,
on a failure to distinguish between two different meanings
of humanism. The first type of humanism sees the human
being as the end-in-itself and as the supreme value. This
type of humanism, exemplified for Sartre in Jean Cocteau's
Round the World in 80 Hours, ascribes value to human beings
according to the most distinguished deeds of great people.
This kind of humanism is absurd and inadmissible, because
such a judgement on the magnificence of humankind could
only be made by someone who stood outside the human race,
such as a dog or a horse. Furthermore, for the existentialist
the human being is never the end, but is always something
which is still to be determined.

The second meaning of humanism is that the human
being has the capacity to project and go beyond himself, and
does so by pursuing aims he himself invents and chooses.
This means there is no other universe except the universe
of human subjectivity, i.e. the universe that human beings
create for themselves. This provides us with the basis for
understanding *existential humanism*. Existential humanism
holds that the human being is constituted by a relation between transcendence and subjectivity. The existentialist uses
the term 'transcendence' not in a religious sense but to express the capacity of human beings to surpass, exceed and
go beyond themselves. By 'subjectivity' the existentialist does
not mean subjectivism, but that the human being is forever
present in a human universe. This view of the human being
as a relation of transcendence and subjectivity is *humanism*,

because *the human being* is the sole legislator for himself and it is he alone who must decide for himself. Furthermore, existentialism is a humanism, because it makes clear that it is always by seeking an aim beyond himself that the human being realizes himself as truly human.

In conclusion, the objections raised against existentialism are unfounded. Existentialism simply attempts to draw the full conclusions that follow from a consistently atheistic position. It does not promote despair. The existentialist conception of despair differs from the Christian understanding, which conceives of despair as 'any attitude of unbelief'. The atheism of existentialism is due not to proving God's non-existence, but to the conviction that God's existence makes no difference to the human being. The real problem is not the existence or non-existence of God but that each human being must take responsibility for himself, must invent and choose his values, and act on those values. Consequently, existentialism is not a doctrine of despair, as Christians mistakenly believe, but is an optimistic doctrine of action.

Sartre's Discussion with Members of the Audience (pp. 57–70)

The first questioner argues that despair, abandonment and anguish are not constant states and do not occur concurrently. Sartre responds by making clear that he is not referring to the trivial choices we make in our everyday lives, like which cake to choose for our dessert, but is referring to the choice that makes each human being the person he or she is. This constant choice of oneself is a choice which is always accompanied by anguish, first, because the choice can never be justified on objective grounds and, second, because in choosing for oneself one is simultaneously choosing what one believes to be right for all human beings and is thus responsible to the whole of humanity. The first questioner replies that he was alluding in his question to Sartre's earlier essay in *Action*, which in his opinion weakens Sartre's argument. Sartre responds by pointing out that existentialism is a philosophy of commitment, and consequently must be 'lived' if it is to be sincere. This is why he has chosen the path of 'popularization', for although popularization may weaken an idea, it is necessary in order to make existentialism intelligible to people so they can understand the commitment it demands and act upon it in their own lives. The questioner's comment implies an old-fashioned view which restricts philosophy to professional philosophers, whereas, as Marx exemplifies, philosophy has now entered the market-place and is of interest to ordinary people.

The questioner responds with the claim that the *Communist Manifesto* was not a popularization but a weapon of war and an act of commitment. There is thus a clear link between Marx's philosophy and political action. There is, however, no such connection between Sartre's philosophy and morality. Sartre responds by arguing that because existentialism is concerned with 'a morality of freedom', no such connection is required. Although in Marx's age commitment meant revolution, in the present age there is a confusing variety of revolutionary parties. In such a context commitment consists in clarifying the conception in order to define the situation, and thereby influence the various revolutionary practices.

Naville begins his lengthy response to Sartre's lecture by raising the question whether Sartre's philosophy is not merely 'the resurrection of radical-socialism', by which he seems to mean a pre-Marxist, outmoded form of socialism based on liberal values. Sartre's version of this 'liberal humanism' differs from older liberalism only in its emphasis on anguish, which reflects the current social crisis of the world. Naville claims that, despite Sartre's distinction between two meanings of 'human condition' and other terms in common use, Sartre still adheres to the older meaning of humanism.

Naville summarizes Sartre's philosophy as the view that the human being 'presents himself as a choice to be made', which means the human being is not determined by a prior human nature but by his present functioning as an individual. Naville claims that Sartre's concept of 'existence' and 'the human condition' are merely a reversion in a new guise to the eighteenth-century conception of human nature. The difference in the modern situation is that because of the disintegration of society and the 'stirring-together of all races and nations', it has become difficult to present a uniform, generalized and universal presentation of human nature. Because of the complexity of the modern situation, the eighteenth-century notion of human nature has been replaced by the concept of the human condition, which because of the current circumstances is presented in a vague, chaotic and dramatic way. This analysis of the current situation applies to existentialism, which according to Naville continues to subscribe to the notion of human nature, but a human nature now understood as fearful, uncertain and forlorn. Naville further comments that by 'human condition' the existentialist means a 'pre-condition' or 'pre-engagement', rather than a commitment or real condition. Sartre also needs to take into consideration the role of history in the human condition, for it is history that makes human beings the distinct individuals they are. It is because human beings have an 'actual history' that they never live in a world that provides them with an abstract human condition, and it is only because human beings have a history that we can speak of the human condition. It is only in this latter sense that it is valid to speak of the human condition as a primary reality. Just as there can be no abstract human nature, so too can there be no general, abstract human condition. Because the human being is a historical entity, it is possible to identify the laws according to which human beings function. It is these laws which constitute human nature.

Naville then turns to the meaning of 'humanism', a term which he claims has been employed to denote a variety of different philosophical tendencies including Marxism, classical rationalism, Christianity, Hinduism, existentialism, indeed religions and philosophies in general. Naville sees these claims to 'humanism' as the reinstatement of a philosophy which refuses to commit itself. Christianity's claim to be 'humanist' is merely the expression of its inability to detach itself from reactionary positions and commit itself to the revolution. The pseudo-Marxists and liberals, on the other hand, emphasize personal rights because they recoil before the exigencies of the present world situation. The same criticism applies to the existentialist, who offers a general account of the human being because he is unable to formulate a position that does justice to current events. For Naville only Marxism is able to address the problems faced by the current age.

Naville's next point is to deny the validity of the existentialist notion of freedom. He does so on two grounds. First, human beings cannot strive for freedom without *knowing* that they are striving for it. Second, human beings can struggle for a cause that overrules their individual freedom, which shows that human beings can act within a frame greater than themselves and not merely individualistically. Furthermore, when the existentialist states that the human being strives for freedom but without being able to indicate the goal towards which the human being should strive, the existentialist is stating that the individual's actions are part of a causal network that he cannot grasp in its entirety, and which consequently prevents him from knowing in advance or being able to predict the results of his actions. Yet at the same time, the existentialist is claiming that it is precisely within this causal network that the individual's freely chosen actions are rounded off and endowed with meaning. For Sartre, however, 'the choice is a pre-choice', which for Naville shows that Sartre is concerned with 'the freedom of a prior indifference'.

Sartre's concepts of human condition and freedom, Naville continues, are dependent upon understanding 'the objective' as a collection of objects at human beings' disposal but which are in frightening discontinuity with human beings. Such a conception of objectivity results in an understanding of the world which is a-causal, arbitrary and in conflict with modern science. This a-causal, arbitrary conception of the world stems from the existentialist's separation of the world and the human condition, whereas the world is in reality an entirety that includes both objects *and* human beings. Sartre's freedom, Naville claims, is derived from an arbitrary contempt for things. It is a mistake to interpret the objective world as being in a relationship of permanent hostility towards human beings, a view which is the very opposite of Marxist materialism.

Sartre is further guilty of denaturing history. Thus Sartre's claim that Marx developed his philosophy because he was committed to it, overlooks the fact that Marx distilled his philosophy out of a multiplicity of experiences. This is evident from the fact that Marx's philosophy arose in conscious connection with developments taking place in politics and society. Even the apparently apolitical philosophies of Kant and Descartes have a political dimension.

For Naville existentialism needs to engage in self-criticism and undergo a dialectical crisis if it is to retain certain positions of value held by some of its supporters. This is especially important in view of the fact that some of its adherents have used existentialism to justify retrograde social positions and to bolster the *petit*-bourgeoisie. Naville is prepared to concede that existentialism does not lead to quietism, but he accuses it of fostering 'attentism', i.e. an attitude of deferring commitment until one has discerned which is the winning side. Such an attitude is incompatible with commitment to collective and prescriptive values. Naville ends his lengthy response to Sartre's lecture by calling on existentialism to give clear guidance to human beings.

Sartre begins his response by pointing out that Naville's critique stems from a dogmatic position. He does not pursue this point, however, but turns to discuss Naville's conception of truth. Naville's critique of existentialism presupposes the belief there are some things that are *absolutely* true. Sartre wishes to know the source of Naville's certitude, for it seems impossible to justify it, if he views all human beings as objects, as Sartre takes Naville's critique to indicate. Naville is also wrong in his claim that it is respect for human dignity that prevents human beings from viewing other human beings as objects. For Sartre there are philosophical and logical grounds for not regarding human beings as objects, namely that truth disappears if we postulate a universe of objects. To justify this claim, Sartre points out that the objective world is the world of the probable and therefore all theories about it are themselves only probable. Evidence for this can be seen in the variety and hypothetical nature of scientific theories. Furthermore,

Naville would seem, on the basis of his own position, to be unable to show that Marx's theory has anything more than theoretical value. Existentialism, however, is able to address such problems by affirming the primacy of subjectivity by deducing rules from the Cartesian *cogito*.

Naville's critique of the notion of a 'human condition' fails to notice that Sartre accepts much of the Marxist position. It is also wrong, Sartre complains, for Naville to compare him with eighteenth-century philosophers, who were ignorant of the issues that existentialism seeks to address. For existentialism the real problem is: since there is no human nature, how can we preserve throughout the continual changes of history universal principles sufficient to interpret past events such as, for example, the phenomenon of Spartacus? Sartre sees himself and Naville as in agreement in denying human nature and holding that each epoch develops according to dialectical laws. It is the epoch in which they live, not 'human nature' upon which human beings depend.

In response Naville points out that we understand the past by drawing analogies and pointing out differences with the present. If we attempted to turn analogy into an abstract, general principle, however, we should arrive at nothing and lose our standard for comparing the present with the past. For Naville, Sartre seems to be claiming that we can analyse the present only on the basis of observations on the human condition in general. Such an abstract conception of the human condition would make it impossible to analyse the past.

Sartre denies that this is his intention and explains that when he speaks of 'situation' he means the whole of the conditions which define an epoch. According to Naville, however, this definition conflicts with Sartre's own writings and is fundamentally different from Marxism, because it denies causality. Sartre's definition is imprecise, while the Marxist view is that a situation is a totality constructed by causal factors, including 'causality of a statistical kind'.

For Sartre the notion of 'causality of a statistical order' is meaningless. He demands a clear definition of causality from Naville, whom he accuses of having a dream about Marxist causality. Naville responds by asking whether Sartre admits the existence of scientific truth, for if this world is only a world of probabilities, then science can never achieve absolute truth but only relative truth. Naville demands that Sartre accept that the sciences employ the notion of causality. Sartre refuses Naville's request on the grounds that the sciences are abstract, and study variations of factors that are equally abstract, and do not deal with real causality. Furthermore, the Marxist notion of causality is not the same as that of science.

Finally, Naville tells Sartre that if a young man had come to him for advice he would have recommended a definite course of action. Sartre responds by arguing that the young man has already chosen his course of action by his choice of adviser.

Glossary

Abandonment. The view that since God does not exist and there are no objective standards to guide human beings, they are alone in deciding which values to live their lives by.

Anguish. The human being's disquiet that there is no objective authority to guide him in exercising his freedom and consequently has to take sole responsibility for his decisions and actions. This anguish is intensified by the responsibility each human being bears for the whole of humankind when he chooses his values, for in choosing these values he is affirming their validity for all human beings.

A priori. A Latin phrase meaning 'from what is prior' or 'from what comes before', which Kant used to denote knowledge that we can acquire independently of experience. Sartre employs the term to refer to the view that there are objective values which all human beings share and are obliged to follow.

Atheism. Rejection of belief in God's existence.

Authenticity. The human being is 'authentic' when he acknowledges his freedom and the responsibility he bears both for himself and for others in acting on this freedom.

Bad faith. The opposite of authenticity. Bad faith is the attempt of the individual to flee from his freedom by refusing to acknowledge responsibility for himself by, for example, excusing his actions on the grounds that he was only 'following orders'. See also determinism.

Bourgeoisie, bourgeois. In Marxist theory the noun *bourgeoisie* and its adjective *bourgeois* denote the social class in modern capitalist society which owns the means of production and lives from the profits produced by the proletariat, i.e. the wage-earning and non-capital owning class.

Cartesianism. A term which denotes the philosophy and philosophical methods developed by the French philosopher René Descartes.

Categorical imperative. The moral law formulated by Kant which

Glossary

states that the human being should act only in accordance with that maxim which he or she can at the same time will as a universal law.

Cocteau, Jean (1889–1963). French poet, writer, artist and film-maker.

Cogito ergo sum. A Latin phrase meaning 'I think, therefore I am', coined by Descartes in his search for a truth that cannot be doubted and can therefore provide a certain and unquestionable foundation for knowledge. Descartes argues that the human being's own exist-ence is the one thing that no human being can doubt. On the basis of this principle Descartes attempts to derive a system of certain knowledge. For Sartre, the importance of the *cogito* is that it ex-presses the insight that philosophy must take as its starting-point the fact that human beings are individual, self-conscious beings.

Commitment. The free individual's engagement and action in the world. Commitment is the means by which the individual realizes himself in committing himself to a type of human existence which he has chosen for himself.

Descartes, René (1596–1650). French philosopher, whose works *Dis-course on Method* and *Meditations on First Philosophy* were highly influential on subsequent philosophy.

Despair. Living without hope in any external power, such as God, human nature, or objective values, to shape our lives for us.

Determinism. The view that human beings do not have free will and that their decisions and actions are regulated by an external power such as God, fate, or heredity. For Sartre determinism is an example of bad faith, for it is an attempt by the individual to evade taking responsibility for his own actions. See also bad faith.

Dostoyevsky, Fyodor (1821–81). Russian author often regarded as a forerunner of existentialism because of his exploration in his novels of such themes as anguish, despair and abandonment.

Eliot, George (1819–80). The *nom de plume* of the English novelist Mary Anne Evans, the author of *Adam Bede, Mill on the Floss, Silas Marner, Middlemarch*, and other novels.

Existence precedes essence. 'Essence' designates the characteristics that make something what it is. For example, the 'essence' of a table is to be a piece of furniture consisting of a flat surface supported by (usually) four legs, The human being, however, is not definable in this way, for the human being is an individual who becomes what he is through the choices he makes. Sartre rejects the view that human beings have a fixed, *a priori* essence which determines what they are. Because they are free, each human being is uniquely what he is through the choices he makes. Sartre expresses this idea in his slogan 'existence precedes essence', by which he means that the human being's existence is not defined in advance, say by God or by an objective human nature which all human beings share, but is determined by each individual through his free decisions and actions.

Existentialism. A term which denotes philosophies, theologies and literature that focus on and attempt to elucidate the concrete existence of the individual human being, especially in situations of crisis such as anxiety, despair, guilt and death. Its chief representatives are Kierkegaard, Heidegger, Jaspers and Sartre.

Freedom. Human beings are free in the sense that each of us is solely responsible for deciding what sort of human beings we are to be. There is no other power which makes our decisions for us and determines what we are. Indeed, human beings are 'condemned to be free', for we have no choice but to choose for ourselves with no external help. Our freedom is not capricious or arbitrary for two reasons. First, freedom is always accompanied by responsibility. This is because when the individual chooses, he chooses not only for himself but for the whole of humankind. Second, the human being always exercises his freedom in a concrete, historical context.

Gide, André (1869–1951). French novelist and literary critic, winner of the Nobel Prize for Literature (1947).

Heidegger, Martin (1889–1976). German philosopher whose *Being and Time* (1927) was highly influential on twentieth-century existentialist philosophy.

Humanism. A diffuse term describing theories which take not God, revelation, or religious authority but the human being as their starting-point. Existentialism is a humanism because it understands the individual human being to be the sole creator of values, meaning and morality.

Idealism. A term used of philosophies which hold that the external world is in some way dependent upon the mind.

Inter-subjectivity. Although human beings are individuals who are responsible for creating themselves through their choices, they do this in the context of other human beings. These other human beings are important for the subjectivity of the individual, for it is in relation to other human beings that the human being makes the decisions that define his own existence. Sartre points out that the recognition of oneself as spiritual, wicked, or jealous is due to the interaction of the self with other selves. Thus although existentialism emphasizes the subjectivity of the individual human being, this does not mean that existentialism is narrowly individualistic and denies the reality or rights of other selves. Although a unique individual, each human being exists in relation to other human beings, who provide the context within which each human being shapes his or her own individual existence.

Jaspers, Karl (1883–1969). German philosopher regarded as one of the founders of twentieth-century existentialism.

Kant, Immanuel (1724–1804). German philosopher whose three 'critiques' (*Critique of Pure Reason, Critique of Practical Reason, Critique of Judgement*) and other works had a profound effect on metaphysics, epistemology, moral philosophy and philosophy of religion.

Kantianism. Any philosophy that is based on, or influenced by, the principles of Kant's critical philosophy.

Kierkegaard, Søren (1813–55). Danish thinker regarded by many as the 'father of existentialism'. The author of such classic existentialist works as *Concept of Anxiety, Concluding Unscientific Postscript* and *Sickness unto Death.*

Macquarrie, John (1919–2007). Scottish Anglican theologian who has drawn on existentialist philosophy, particularly that of Martin Heidegger, as a resource for developing a modern philosophical theology.

Marcel, Gabriel (1889–1973). French Roman Catholic existentialist philosopher and friend of Sartre, who according to Simone de Beauvoir coined the term 'existentialism' to describe Sartre's philosophy.

Materialism. The view that everything is either made of matter or ultimately derived from matter.

Morality. A set of principles prescribing what is right and wrong, and how human beings should behave. Sartre rejects the notion of an objective morality that exists independently of human beings and argues for a subjective morality that each human being freely chooses for himself.

Naturalism. The view that everything is 'natural' and that there is no need to look beyond nature for explanations of the world and our place in it. With regard to ethics the term denotes the view that ethical values can be derived from non-ethical, natural premises or are natural properties.

Glossary

Nihilism. The critique and sometimes rejection of morality on the grounds that there are no compelling arguments that can irrefutably justify the validity of moral values. One of the aims Sartre set himself in *Existentialism and Humanism* was to refute the claim that existentialism is nihilistic.

Objectivity. The view that moral values exist independently of the feelings of individual human beings and are guaranteed by some external power or criterion such as God, human nature, reason, or natural law.

Phenomenology. A philosophical method developed by the German philosopher Edmund Husserl (1859–1938) which studies the structures of consciousness by investigating 'phenomena', i.e. the appearances things have in human experience. Phenomenology attempts to identify the essences of mental acts common to different minds by 'bracketing' or excluding the objective world. It thus takes the subjective consciousness or first-person point of view as the starting-point for philosophizing.

Project. The human being is a 'project' for two reasons. First, as long as he lives the human being is never a finished product but a work in progress. Second, because the human being has the capacity to make and remake himself through his decisions and actions, the human being is a being that throws itself forwards or 'pro-jects' itself into the future.

Quietism. Resignation, passivity and inactivity in the face of the fact that there are no objective guarantees to support or justify our decisions and actions.

Stendhal (1783–1842). The *nom de plume* of the French writer Marie-Henri Beyle, responsible for such classics of French literature as *Le Rouge et le Noir* (The Red and the Black) and *La Chartreuse de Parme* (The Charterhouse of Parma).

Subjectivity. The condition of being a subject, which for Sartre is the basis for the individual's choice of moral values. It is the individual subject who freely chooses his or her values, not some allegedly objective power or criterion such as God or human nature. Furthermore, since, as Descartes has shown, the human being's own self-consciousness is the only thing that the human being cannot doubt, subjectivity is the most appropriate starting-point for philosophy.

Transcendence. Human beings do not have a fixed, unchanging nature, but have the ability to go beyond, surpass, or 'transcend' what they are now by reinventing themselves through their decisions, choices and actions.

Glossary

Zola, Émile (1840–1902). French novelist whose novels focused on the effects of heredity and environment on moral responsibility.